T0326980

The HOT BROWN

The HOT BROWN

Louisville's Legendary Open-Faced Sandwich

ALBERT W. A. SCHMID

RED ⚡ LIGHTNING BOOKS

This book is a publication of

Red Lightning Books
1320 East 10th Street
Bloomington, Indiana 47405 USA

redlightningbooks.com

© 2018 by Albert W.A. Schmid

Manufactured in the United States of America

ISBN 978-1-68435-005-6 (cl.)
ISBN 978-1-68435-006-3 (ebk.)

1 2 3 4 5   23 22 21 20 19 18

CONTENTS

FOREWORD

Baptized by Bubbling Mornay

WHEN I WROTE A BOOK on country ham several years ago, my mother said after reading it, "I'd never thought anyone could write an entire book on something so simple as that."

That same thought occurred to me in the summer of 2016 when Albert Schmid told me he was working on a book about the Hot Brown, the legendary hot sandwich and/or bubbling casserole named after the Brown Hotel in Louisville, Kentucky. Turkey, cheesy Mornay, bacon, tomato, toast, and off you go. Cut and dried, stick-to-your-ribs sustenance at its best.

Or blandest, depending on which version you ate. And there are countless examples of truly dreadful Hot Browns right here in the Derby City.

I first encountered a bad version of a Hot Brown when I was a kid. My senior citizen neighbor across the street from my home made what she called a Hot Brown for her husband. I happened to be in the kitchen as she was plating their dinner one evening, and though I had no sound culinary experience at that time, I judged this dish wholly unsuitable. (OK, "just plain gross" was what I thought, 'cause I was a kid.) The assemblage began with a slice of white bread browned to brittle-dry by a toaster, then topped with sliced deli turkey, followed by a pair of bacon slices placed in an X formation and glued onto the bread with a melted slice of American cheese.

The thin slice of tomato she used to garnish the dish looked more wound-like than appetizing.

Years later, in my first cook's job, the Hot Brown reappeared. And despite it being on the menu at what then was a swell Louisville restaurant, it was hardly better. A shockingly dry and bland disk of Holland rusk was the dish's bread base, and cheap deli sliced turkey and country ham shavings represented the protein center. It was topped with a solid cheddar Mornay, then garnished with sliced scallions and bacon. The result was gooey and odd: the desiccated bread sucked up much of the sauce's moisture, and the combination of country ham and scallions was, well, just weird. The four thousand or so of those I admit to cooking in that kitchen only strengthened my resolve to never eat one myself.

Fast forward to 2011, when Adam Richman, host of *Man vs. Food*, visited Louisville to make the Hot Brown with then Brown Hotel executive chef, Laurent Geroli. The chef's combination started with Texas toast, coarse chunks of fresh roasted turkey breast, a Pecorino-Romano Mornay built on a cream-only béchamel, wedges of tomato, and bacon. Transfixed and with my mouth watering, I mumbled to my wife, "I'm going to get one of those." One week later, I did, and I was an instant fan. Hearing Geroli chide me in his French Canadian accent, "Vwhat tooook you so long, hein? I told you zees was good, no?" was worth it. I was so engrossed in the dish, this molten garden of caloric delights, that he could have disparaged my family name and I'd have nodded affirmatively.

Ever since that edible epiphany, I've seen Hot Browns not only everywhere on dozens of Louisville menus, but even some renditions at spots well out of town. I've seen a basic mirror of the traditional version in lots of places, but I've also seen Hot Brown pizzas, Hot Brown-loaded fries, Hot Brown

Eggs Benedict, Hot Brown soups, and even Hot Brown salads. Given chefs' drive to create variations on themes, I'm confident that Hot Brown nachos, Hot Brown pho, and molecular deconstructed Hot Brown options are on their way. But the original . . . the one created in 1926 for crowds who danced late, so late into the night that they were miserably hungry . . . the one for which the hotel has gained well-deserved fame and subsequently charges a premium price . . . that's the one, folks, the real McCoy, the bomb. And to the credit of the Brown Hotel, the recipe for this culinary jewel is on its website, there for the taking, but yours for the making.

Were my mother in this conversation, I'd be defending my friend, Albert, author of this book, saying, "Yes, Mom, there's enough cool stuff surrounding the Hot Brown to write a book, and I bet you'll like it when you read it." And as you delve into the pages chockful of stories about this cherished, cheesy dish, I think you'll agree, too.

Steve Coomes, 2017
Louisville, Kentucky

A former chef turned food, spirits, and travel writer, Steve Coomes is author of *Country Ham: A Southern Tradition of Hogs, Salt & Smoke*. He lives in Louisville, Kentucky.

PREFACE

I DEVOURED MY FIRST HOT Brown sandwich at a lunch during a long weekend visit to Louisville when I interviewed for a chef-instructor position at Sullivan University's National Center for Hospitality Studies (NCHS) early in 1999. I traveled from Maryville, Missouri, where I was the executive chef at Northwest Missouri State University, with the hopes that I would impress the Sullivan team enough that they would offer me a job. Once I arrived in Louisville, I transferred from the airport to my hotel, a Holiday Inn that would, many years later, be acquired by Sullivan University and transformed into a student dorm now known as Gardiner Point. The "interview" consisted of multiple mini-interviews over several days with many members of the faculty and administration at Sullivan University, finishing with a grand dinner at Winston's, at the time the campus restaurant, with all the department heads of the NCHS, including Dean Newal Hunter, Kerry Sommerville, chair of Hotel-Restaurant Management, Chef Tom Hickey chair of Culinary Arts, Chef Derek Spendlove, chair of Baking & Pastry, Chef Kim Jones, chair of Catering as well as Chef Mik Milster, a Culinary Arts instructor. The meal was cooked by Winston's executive chef, John Castro. The food and the company made the evening experience memorable. We talked, ate, laughed, and enjoyed each other's company. Each of us is now following our own path in various parts of the United States.

Earlier that weekend, Chef Jones, a longtime Louisvillian, and I had a working lunch, during which she conducted her part of the interview. She asked where I would like to eat—I responded the way I always respond when I am visiting an area I'm unfamiliar with, "somewhere local." She asked if I had ever had a Hot Brown sandwich. When I answered "no," she said, "Well—your trip to Louisville will not be complete without a Hot Brown!" Then she drove me to a local restaurant that had the Hot Brown on the menu. I would later realize that even though this sandwich was invented at the Brown Hotel, most restaurants in Louisville have some iteration of the Hot Brown on their menus. When the Hot Brown arrived at the table the tomatoes were slightly shriveled from the heat of the broiler. The bacon looked crisp, and the Mornay sauce was bubbling. The aroma of the Hot Brown was heavenly . . . and devilish. The first bite was rich, creamy, and delicious. The Hot Brown was very easy to eat because all the flavors complemented each other so well. I ate the whole sandwich before the interview was over. I spoke with Kim recently, and she described the Hot Brown as an "iconic dish" known all over the United States and all over the world. In fact, she enjoyed a Hot Brown at the Brown Derby at Hollywood Studios at Disney World on Derby Day, 2017.

By the end of the weekend, I thought that the interviews had gone very well, and I hoped that the powers that be at Sullivan University were going to offer me a teaching position. I was thrilled that the offer was delivered by Dean Hunter before I boarded the plane back to Missouri. I was honored to join the accomplished faculty of the National Center for Hospitality Studies. I spent the next eighteen years teaching at Sullivan University in the culinary arts, hotel-restaurant management, hospitality management, and beverage management departments. Wow! What great memories!

Over the almost two decades I spent in Louisville, I consumed more than my weight in Hot Browns, many of them at the Brown Hotel. There is nothing like eating a Hot Brown at the Brown Hotel. The hotel itself is grand. I have eaten Hot Browns in J. Graham's, the ground floor eatery, and at the Lobby Bar—both venues were fantastic for consuming a Hot Brown! Over the years, I have been fortunate to travel extensively. I have enjoyed food and drink at many grand hotels all over the world, but very few foods that were developed in hotels are as iconic as the Hot Brown.

In 2016, I was offered and assumed the position of director of the culinary arts and hospitality management departments at Guilford Technical Community College in Jamestown, North Carolina, which is a very cool small town that is sandwiched between Greensboro and High Point. Jamestown has an incredible food scene for a town its size. We have an oyster bar, a Southern cuisine restaurant (which features a gluten-free menu), a specialty beer and wine store, a free-standing bakery, and an incredible culinary school at the local community college—although I might be a little biased about the culinary school. I am now building new memories and experiences with the excellent faculty at GTCC—I left one exemplary faculty to grow with another exemplary faculty. The interview at Sullivan University was well over twenty years ago. I hope that my next twenty years are just as exciting and fulfilling at my new home. But I hope I never forget that weekend in Louisville or that first Hot Brown.

Cheers,
Albert W. A. Schmid
Greensboro, North Carolina

ACKNOWLEDGMENTS

THE AUTHOR WISHES TO THANK: His wife, Kim, for her love, support, advice, and for providing the primary editing on this manuscript, and his sons, Tom and Mike, for their support on all his projects.

His parents, Thomas and Elizabeth Schmid, father in-law, Richard Dunn, and his brother and sisters and their families, Gretchen, Tiffany, Rachel, Justin, Bennett, Ana, Shane, and John, for all your support.

The awesome culinary and hospitality team at Guilford Technical Community College (GTCC), Linda Bietz, Keith Gardiner, Tom Lantz, Al Romano, L. J. Rush, Michele Prairie, and Patrick Saneki, thank you for your support, friendship, and for making me look good! Also, to Kathy King—enjoy your retirement!

Brad Walker, the general manager of the Brown Hotel, and Marc Salmon, the HR director of the Brown Hotel—without your support and help, this project would not have been completed.

David Dominé, fellow author, whose insight and opinions on the Hot Brown helped to focus me.

Sam Mudd, former colleague and fellow chef, who taught me to miniaturize the Hot Brown sandwich.

Jessica Ebelhar for the amazing picture on the cover and for assisting in the research regarding Chef Fred K. Schmidt.

Loreal "the Butcher Babe" Gavin for your friendship and support.

Dr. Randy Parker, president of GTCC for leading the institution where I teach and allowing me to continue to write.

Dr. Beth Pitonzo, vice president of instruction and Sheila May, associate vice president of instruction, for your support and guidance.

Rich Depolt and Samuel Richardson III, for your leadership and guidance of the GTCC division in which I teach.

Music, including that of Justin Timberlake, Bruno Mars, Jay-Z, Alicia Keys, Stacey Kent, Bebel Gilberto, Oscar Peterson, Gary Allen, Keb-Mo, Raul Malo, Frank Sinatra, Glenn Miller, and Quincy Jones, that the author listened to while writing this book.

The HOT BROWN

ONE

The Hot Brown Sandwich

THE HOT BROWN SANDWICH IS an inspired culinary creation that helped to put Kentucky cuisine on the map as one of the many great cuisines in the United States. The Hot Brown sandwich, known to locals as a "Hot Brown" was created as a late fall to winter sandwich. "I never cease to be amazed that people will drive hundreds of miles (to the Brown Hotel) for a Hot Brown," said Brad Walker, the general manager and vice president of the Brown Hotel for the past fifteen years and graduate from Cornell's hotel and restaurant management program. Later in the interview, Walker referred to the culinary creation as "our lovely little sandwich." The Hot Brown attracts people from outside the hotel. Walker said it is not uncommon for "six, eight, ten people to show up at J. Graham's Café and all of them order a Hot Brown." They come from all over the United States and even overseas says Walker, who knows this fact because people post their experience on social media. "Hotels (in the Louisville area) will direct people to the Brown for a Hot Brown," said Walker, who added that other hotels directing people away from their hotel to benefit another hotel is a unique situation that does not always happen. "The Welcome Center also sends a lot our way."

The Hot Brown is most likely a variation of the Welsh rarebit, although Kentucky author David Dominé observed in an interview, "I have always wondered if the Hot Brown was inspired by the Croque-Monsieur, just deconstructed." This theory stands up to scrutiny as the croque monsieur first appeared on a Paris café menu in 1910. Some soldiers from the United States would have seen this sandwich before returning home at the end of the Great War (World War I). Also, the croque monsieur is mentioned in Marcel Proust's 1919 novel, À la recherche du temps perdu: À lombre des jeunes filles en fleurs (*In Search of Lost Time: In the Shadow of Young Girls in Flower*), the second in his seven-novel masterwork. Of course, perhaps the Welsh rarebit, a sandwich dating back to sometime in the early sixteenth century, spawned the croque monsieur, which spawned the Hot Brown. Or, perhaps a direct line can be drawn from the Welsh rarebit to the Hot Brown. No one really knows for sure. In any case, the Hot Brown was invented at the Brown Hotel in 1926 by Chef Fred K. Schmidt during the height of Prohibition.[1]

Since its creation, the Hot Brown has gained worldwide fame and has been featured in newspaper articles and on television shows, and the recipe is found in many Kentucky cuisine cookbooks not to mention many other cookbooks. In fact, a Kentucky cookbook without a Hot Brown is incomplete. An incredible public relations effort and notoriety surround this open-faced sandwich, that was most likely made from nothing more than kitchen scraps—as something warm to eat on a frigid winter night during a break from dancing on the roof top at the Brown Hotel in Louisville, Kentucky, as an alternative to ham and eggs. Although another story has the Hot Brown being created to ward off a patron's hangover—which seems unlikely since the sandwich was created in the middle of Prohibition. Of course, Prohibition stopped very few people from imbibing in the United States, much less in Kentucky, the home of many bourbon distilleries. The Brown Hotel and the Hot Brown survived the Great Depression too. The sandwich gained so much notoriety that by the 1940s, many customers entered the Brown Hotel restaurant with their mind made up about what they were going to order, and many never looked at the other offerings on the menu.[2] "This happens even today, especially on the weekends," said Marc Salmon, director of human resources at the Brown Hotel.

Even though the Hot Brown is now served year round, there is evidence that this sandwich was originally created for the frosty winter months and that another creation, the Cold Brown, was created for the sweltering summer months. If the original intent of Chef Schmidt was to create a hot signature sandwich, the timing for access to turkey could not have been better planned, as turkey is the favored bird for the United States' Thanksgiving holiday. Many people use leftovers to make Hot Browns during the weekend after Thanksgiving. When Chef Schmidt created the sandwich as a "special" to use up leftovers (the chef was being efficient with what was on hand in the kitchen—something a good chef is trained to do to reduce the food cost in the kitchen), he stumbled on an instant classic. The Hot Brown has become one of the comfort food staples of Kentucky cuisine available at Louisville restaurants, even when the Brown Hotel was closed from February 1971 to 1985. However, what started as a hot open-faced sandwich smothered in sauce has become, often, a concept rather than a classic dish because the original recipe for the Hot Brown is lost to history, and because of the number of Hot Brown dishes that look very different from the original. In fact, "the original Hot Brown was quite different from today's version," reads the narrative before the Hot Brown recipe in *Kentucky Hospitality: A 200-year*

Tradition. Sometime after 1985, with some careful research, the Brown Hotel restored the recipe to a close approximation of the original.[3] Few culinary dishes have lasted as long or have enjoyed as much popularity. Today when someone orders a Hot Brown they can expect turkey on top of bread, covered in Mornay sauce, and topped with wedges of tomato and two slices of bacon. The sandwich is so important to the identity of the Brown that "every employee needs to be able to describe the Hot Brown," says Mark Salmon, "so we serve the sandwich and discuss it in new employee orientation." Many restaurants offer their own twist to this classic sandwich, sometimes substituting one of the elements of the sandwich for something else or by adding something new. Each element of this sandwich is important and together they are an outstanding feast!

The following are the main elements of the Hot Brown. These ingredients together make the perfect sandwich and a filling meal. Chef Bobby Flay once said, "The only thing bad about a Hot Brown is that you need a nap right after you eat it."

Turkey or Chicken (Meat or Protein)

Sliced or broken pieces of turkey breast meat (or sometimes chicken breast) is most commonly used in Hot Brown recipes. Hot Browns are a wonderful use for leftover turkey. In fact, many Kentucky families enjoy Hot Browns the day after Thanksgiving while watching football. The amount of turkey varies from recipe to recipe, but this protein plays the leading role so an average of three to four ounces should be used to make one sandwich. The turkey should be broken up by hand and minimally sliced to make sure that the turkey stays in as natural a shape as possible. Processed turkey slices are discouraged in most recipes and make a very different final dish. Some riffs on the Hot Brown sandwich use other protein choices, which then leads to a name change. For example, the Pattie Brown that uses beef, and the Not Brown that includes seafood.

Bacon

Bacon plays a supporting role in the Hot Brown and serves as a garnish for the sandwich. If the Hot Brown was a feature film, bacon would win an "Oscar"—or perhaps a "Julia" since we are discussing food—for its performance in completing the Hot Brown. In the United States, most bacon comes from the belly of a pig and is usually heavily marbled with fat and smoked with a hardwood such as apple, hickory, or mesquite, although some bacon makers in North America use corn cobs to smoke their bacon. Other countries have leaner cuts of bacon that come from the back of the pig. The amount of bacon served on a Hot Brown is one of the elements that almost everyone agrees upon: each Hot Brown should receive at least two slices of bacon, but feel free to add as much bacon as your arteries can handle.

Tomato (or Fruit)

The tomato is a latecomer to the Hot Brown recipe, which may explain the variations on this ingredient that are sometimes used.[4] If asked, most people would identify the tomato as a vegetable, but the tomato is a fruit. So, it is no surprise that some recipes substitute another fruit, such as the peach, for the tomato. Mark Salmon from the Brown Hotel says, "Peaches are not acceptable on a Hot Brown." Mushrooms, shallots, pimientos, and even peas can also be used in different versions of the sandwich as garnishes, like the croque monsieur, which when garnished with a tomato becomes a croque Provençal. For the Hot Brown, the fruit can be sliced or wedged. Some recipes call for cherry tomatoes while others call for heirloom tomatoes. The creative chef and home cook alike can vary this element of the Hot Brown for unique results in the final dish. Chef Joe Castro, former executive chef at the Brown Hotel, said that the addition of the tomato (or fruit) is important because the acid balances out the dish. If you plan to substitute another fruit or vegetable for the tomato, make sure that your fruit has enough acid to balance out the dish. The Brown Hotel utilizes the Roma tomato to produce Hot Browns.

Toast (Bread)

The bread for the Hot Brown is usually soft, thickly cut white bread like Texas toast that has been toasted lightly, but the bread can be varied with superior results. The Brown Hotel trims the crust from the bread, but there are many restaurants that leave the crust on the bread. Chef Bobby Flay used savory French toast for his Hot Brown, which shows how one might be creative in making the sandwich. Almost any bread can be used to vary the Hot Brown. A simple substitution might include wheat bread, English muffin, flatbread, egg bread, or biscuits. A more complex substitution might use the bread to enrobe the sandwich so that you can carry it as you travel from one place to another.

Mornay Sauce

Mornay sauce is now the accepted sauce to top a Hot Brown, however, it may not have been the original choice of sauce. According to J. B. Hart, one of Chef Schmidt's line cooks, the Mornay sauce was laced with hollandaise sauce. Hollandaise sauce is an emulsified combination of egg yolks, clarified butter, lemon juice, and spices. The original sauce was not featured on the sandwich for long because a few intoxicated customers became sick after eating a Hot Brown. The health department investigated and did not approve of the method of separating eggs with bare hands, according to Hart. So, Chef Schmidt, James G. Brown, and general manager Harold

Harter agreed to remove the hollandaise sauce from the mixture. It is very unlikely that they removed hollandaise sauce completely from the menu because at the time, hollandaise sauce was a staple on many menus in hotels and restaurants. But for the Hot Brown, Chef Schmidt returned to the drawing board, fortifying the Mornay sauce with heavy cream and egg yolk.[5]

Mornay sauce is a classic derivative, or small sauce, of the mother sauce in French classic cuisine, Béchamel (white sauce). The white sauce is basically a fancy milk gravy named Béchamel for King Louis XIV's chief steward, Louis de Béchameil. This mother sauce is considered the easiest to prepare. Originally, the Mornay sauce would have been based upon the velouté sauce as the Béchamel sauce had yet to be created. Per Master Chef Auguste Escoffier, Béchamel is made with white roux, boiling milk, minced onion, lean veal and salt, pepper, nutmeg, and thyme. According to Escoffier the sauce is transformed from Béchamel to Mornay with the fortification of a fumet made from the meat in the dish, in this case turkey, and the addition of Gruyère and Parmesan cheeses and finished with butter. However, too much cheese will make the sauce stringy.[6] Some versions of the Mornay sauce include other cheeses, such as cheddar, cream cheese, American cheese, and Swiss cheese. "Part of the secret is in the sauce," says Walker, "None tastes like ours does." The Brown Hotel uses cream and pecorino cheeses to make their Mornay, making the sauce rich and unique. "We have one person in charge of making the sauce so that the sauce is consistent," says Walker, who added that the Brown Hotel can't delegate the sauce making to many other people because "We don't want a lot of people with their hands in the pot." Mornay sauce may have been named after Philippe, Duc de Mornay, however, the origin of the name is still debated. Chef John Castro, my former colleague at Sullivan University's

National Center for Hospitality Studies and former executive chef at Winston's Restaurant, once referred to Mornay sauce as "cheese gravy," which sums up the classic sauce. However, the staff at the Brown Hotel are forbidden to refer to the sauce in such casual terms.

This recipe for Mornay Sauce is a good starter for the home chef who is new to making the Hot Brown. This recipe is an adaptation on the Béchamel recipe from the James Beard award–winning author of James Peterson's Cooking.[7] *I have adjusted the recipe and added cheese to move the sauce from Béchamel to Mornay.*

ORNAY SAUCE

Makes 1 pint or 4 ½-cup servings
2 tablespoons butter, melted
2 tablespoons flour
2 cups of milk (or cream)
3 tablespoons carrots, small dice
2 tablespoons celery, small dice
¼ cup onion, small dice
2 tablespoons lean ham
1 bay leaf
6 peppercorns
1 teaspoon salt
¼ teaspoon white pepper
1 pinch cayenne pepper
1 pinch nutmeg
½ to ¾ cup cheese, grated

In a small saucepan, bring the milk to a boil, then remove from the burner. Add the onions, carrots, celery, lean ham, bay leaf, and peppercorns. Cover and allow to sit for 15 minutes. Then strain the milk into a container and refrigerate.

Melt the butter in a different saucepan. Once the butter is melted, add the flour and mix the two together until a paste forms. Cook this roux for a very brief period—until it begins to boil—then pour in the cooled, infused milk.

Stir the sauce over medium heat until a gravy forms, and allow the gravy to bubble. Season the sauce with the salt, white pepper, cayenne pepper, and nutmeg. Then add the ½ to ¾ cup of cheese and allow the cheese to melt into the sauce. Once the cheese is melted, the sauce is ready to serve or use on a Hot Brown.

Or, if you want a very simple, creamy cheese sauce, you might try this one that I adapted from Richard Hougen's cream sauce which appears in his first book, Look No Further. *Hougen was a professor of hotel management at Berea College, the manager of the Boone Tavern Hotel, and author of three books. His cream sauce recipe was very important to his cooking, and the recipe is featured in each of his books,* Look No Further, Cooking with Hougen, *and* More Hougen Favorites.[8] *This sauce is a thick sauce and thus perfect for the Hot Brown sandwich.*

$\mathscr{C}$HEESE SAUCE

4 tablespoons flour
4 tablespoons butter
2 cups milk
¼ teaspoon salt
A few grains of pepper
½ cup cheese of your choice, grated

Melt the butter and add the flour. Stir while cooking for about three minutes. Make sure the roux does not brown. Add milk and continue stirring while cooking until the sauce begins to thicken. Season to taste. Hougen states that this is a thick cream sauce and advises adding an additional ½ cup of milk to make the sauce "medium thick" or an additional 1 cup of milk to make a thin sauce.[9]

TWO

People, Places, and Things (and the Legendary Hot Brown)

James Graham Brown

People from outside the Kentucky area might know the name James Graham Brown because of the James Graham Brown Cancer Center or the James Graham Brown Foundation. A Hoosier by birth and a graduate of Hanover College, a small private Presbyterian four-year college in southeast Indiana (the oldest private college in the state), one might think that lifelong bachelor James Graham Brown might leave his wealth to benefit people north of the Ohio River, but when he moved to Louisville in 1903, there was no looking back. He co-owned a lumber company with his father and brother and started to develop downtown Louisville. The name on some of the buildings in downtown Louisville, including the Brown Hotel, the Brown Theater, the Brown garage, and the Martin Brown building, to name a few, suggest who is responsible for constructing them. He also helped to establish the Louisville Zoo, supported the Boy Scouts of America, and provided many donations and grants to schools, universities, and hospitals. Brown lived in the hotel. When he passed away, his wealth, over a hundred million dollars, was set aside in a trust and continues to help the people of Louisville. When he passed, he was the wealthiest man in Kentucky. Brown is buried in Cave Hill Cemetery.

The Brown Hotel

The Brown Hotel is named for the hotel's original owner and creator, James Graham Brown. One of the top hotels in the region with a four-diamond ranking, the Brown Hotel is a historic hotel, founded in 1923. It sits at the corner of Broadway and Fourth Street in downtown Louisville. With over 294 guestrooms and suites, the Brown Hotel is still one of the first choices of people visiting Louisville on business or for the Kentucky Derby. Visitors can dine in J. Graham's Café which is located on the street level. For those guests who don't think they can consume a whole Hot Brown, the café offers a buffet that includes portions of a Hot Brown casserole, and it will also allow two guests to split the Hot Brown between two plates at no extra charge. Guests can order a Hot Brown at the Brown Hotel's premier restaurant, the English Grill, or at the Lobby Bar which are both located on the second floor near the hotel lobby. The bar features an original cocktail: the Muhammad Ali Smash.

Chef Fred Schmidt

Very little is published about Chef Fred Schmidt. According to Marc Salmon, Rudy Suck was the general manager of the Brown Hotel during the 1920s. Also according to Salmon, Mr. Suck recalled that the hotel was looking for something new to serve when the band took its midnight break. Chef Schmidt had an idea for an open-faced turkey sandwich smothered in Mornay sauce. Mr. Suck said the creation sounded "a little flat." The maître d' added that the sandwich should have a little color. Chef Schmidt solved the color problem by adding bacon and placing the sandwich under the broiler. Mr. Suck also suggested the addition of pimientos. (David Dominé says that pimientos would have been a kitchen staple during the 1920s and 1930s to "add a splash of color" and were very familiar to both Suck and Schmidt.) Thus, the creation of the Hot Brown might have been a group effort.

In 1939, Schmidt was interviewed by the *Courier-Journal*. He said that men and women can both be good cooks. "Cooking is not an art. It is not something that one person has a talent for and another has not. Cooking is a mechanical process involving knowledge of the chemistry of food. It is a matter of knowing what will happen under given circumstances and how to combine foods and get desired results." Chef Schmidt went on to say,

> Tell me what a man eats today and I will tell you how he will think tomorrow. If he is prosperous and eats good food, his demands for life are higher and tomorrow he will ascend the scale of better living; he will think in terms of better things. If, however, a depression hits him and he discovers after a while that he must reduce his food budget, he will do so gradually. What he eats today will determine his status tomorrow. With his finances slipping he will think in terms of poorer quality in food, in clothing and in housing. Thus, he will live and think in terms of lower values.[1]

Chef Fred K. Schmidt (1881–1958) was interred at the Resthaven Memorial Cemetery off Bardstown Road. His wife Frances (1903–1978) joined him in 1978. Chef Schmidt was forty-five years old when he helped to invent the Hot Brown and seventy-seven when he passed away. Chef Schmidt's wife and son, Fred Jr., were interviewed in a 1985 article for the

Courier-Journal. The young Schmidt said he "didn't grow up on convenience foods or canned things," implying that his father would have used only natural ingredients to create this classic sandwich. So it was very unlikely that Chef Schmidt would have used processed American cheese. As for the many versions of the Hot Brown, Schmidt Jr. added, "It's like a Reuben, you can do what you want and they're going to."[2]

One for the Record Books

Just a few weeks before the 125th running of the Kentucky Derby in 1999, BiScotty Bistro in La Grange attempted to make the largest Hot Brown ever with the hopes they would impress the editors of the *Guinness Book of World Records*. The mammoth 65-pound sandwich measured 56 by 28 inches and was 3 inches deep. It used "10 loaves of bread, 16 pounds of sliced turkey, 3 gallons of parmesan cheese sauce, 200 tomato slices and 1½ pounds of cooked bacon." A review of the Guinness World Records website did not result in a current record holder for the Hot Brown sandwich. But, in 1999, the restaurant owner, Donna Miller, was quoted as saying, "We had a heck of a good time putting it together."[3] According to the *Courier-Journal* article, it took five people twenty minutes to assemble the sandwich after each of the ingredients was heated. (Ingredients needed to be heated separately because there was no pan or oven big enough to hold the sandwich.) The entire process took over three hours.

Diane Sawyer Visits the Brown Hotel

ABC news anchor Diane Sawyer is a Kentucky native and a graduate of Louisville's Seneca High School. She returned to Louisville to speak with Brown Hotel general manager Brad Walker and restaurant manager Neil Ward. During the interview, Ward told Sawyer that 1.4 million Hot Browns have been served over the years at the Brown Hotel.

Man vs. the Hot Brown

Adam Richman studied to be an actor at the Yale School of Drama but is better known for hosting *Man vs. Food* where he would try to consume plates of "big food" in different towns and cities across the United States. During each episode, Richman would talk about the dish he was about to consume and the restaurant and the people that made the dish. Then he would sit down and try to consume a dish that weighed five pounds or more. When Richman visited the Brown Hotel, he divulged the Brown Hotel recipe's use of cream instead of milk in the Mornay sauce, two pieces of bacon, and two wedges of beefsteak tomato. He referred to the Hot Brown as "without question one of my favorite comfort foods in the world" and said at the end of the segment, "You can't beat an authentic Hot Brown at the legendary Brown Hotel."

The Hot Brown Throwdown!

Chef Robert William "Bobby" Flay was trained at the French Culinary Institute in New York and has spent most of his career in New York. Flay was the host of *Throwdown! with Bobby Flay* for eight seasons; the series ran from 2006 to 2010. The premise of the show was that Flay would surprise an unsuspecting chef who was preparing a regional favorite for a fake Food Network show. Flay would then challenge the chef to a "throwdown," cooking the regional dish. At the end of the second season, Flay challenged Chef Joe Castro, executive chef at the Brown Hotel and his brother, Chef John Castro, executive chef at Winston's Restaurant at Sullivan University's National Center for Hospitality Studies. Both Castro brothers have lived in the Kentucky area most of their lives. During the episode Flay said, "Delicious! I love Kentucky Hot Brown. It's just, sort of, the perfect comfort sandwich." Flay also revealed that he serves a version of the Hot Brown at his restaurant in New York for lunch every day—and that the Hot Brown is the best-selling dish during that meal. Chef Todd Richards, the executive chef at the Seelbach Hotel and Robin Garr of LouisvilleBites.com served as the judges for the Throwdown. Chef Flay started his Hot Brown with a savory French toast topped with turkey, a grilled tomato, sharp cheddar and Parmesan cheese sauce, and applewood-smoked bacon. The Castro brothers prepared a traditional Hot Brown like the one made at the Brown Hotel. In what Garr described as a photo finish—one that Chef Richards said was decided by the bread—the Castro brothers won the day! The Castro chefs were awarded a bottle of Woodford Reserve by Master Distiller Chris Morris of Brown-Forman, and they gained bragging rights.

Hot Brown on the Mind of a Chef

The Public Broadcasting Service (PBS) series, *The Mind of a Chef*, featured a discussion about the Hot Brown with self-admitted hung-over hosts Chef David Chang and Chef Sean Brock, both James Beard award–winning chefs, who explain that the Hot Brown was the perfect sandwich for their situation: "The Hot Brown brought me down!" said Brock.

The Hot Brown Tops the *National Geographic* Top Food Cities List

National Geographic named the Hot Brown and Louisville one of the top ten international food cities in January 2015. Of all places in the world—Louisville, Kentucky! Of all dishes, the Hot Brown! Three cities in the United States were featured, including Kentucky neighbor Cincinnati, Ohio, for their three-way, four-way, and five-way chili, and Buffalo, New York, and its classic bar food, Buffalo wings. Of the other seven cities on the top ten cities list, the only other city from North America was Ensenada, Mexico, with fish tacos.

European members included Lyon, France, for Lyonnaise potatoes, Bologna, Italy, for pasta Bolognese, and Edam, The Netherlands, for Edam cheese. The last three cities on the list are from the far east and included Chennai, India (Chicken 65), Ho Chi Minh City, Vietnam (bánh mì sandwich), and Osaka, Japan (takoyaki).

Kentucky Life

Kentucky Educational Television (KET) broadcast a feature on how to make a Hot Brown with my former student Ryan O'Driscoll explaining the process. The video also features Marc Salmon, the human resources director at the Brown Hotel. Salmon explained that many people passing through Louisville stop at the Brown specifically for the Hot Brown.

Haute Brown . . . $90 Hot Brown

Early in 2016, the Brown Hotel announced that in honor of the Hot Brown's ninetieth birthday, Executive Chef Josh Bettis would offer an updated "Haute Brown." The dish included "turkey roulade wrapped in thick-cut Kentucky bacon accented by tomato confit and roasted tomato gelee, seared foie gras, shaved Parmigiano-Reggiano and house made brioche croutons wrapped with edible gold on top of a white truffle-infused Mornay sauce." The Brown staff suggested a bourbon pairing with a flight of 15-, 20-, and 23-year-old Pappy Van Winkle. For the ultimate experience, the staff at the Brown suggested an overnight stay in the Brown's Muhammad Ali Suite.

*There are many recipes for the Hot Brown but only one that
is produced in the Brown Hotel's kitchens—and here is the
recipe, courtesy of the Brown Hotel. You might want to pause
here, move to the kitchen and make this recipe . . . you won't
regret the effort. Make sure that you don't substitute any
of the ingredients, and follow the directions very carefully
so that you recreate this updated version of the classic dish.
Of course, if you are watching your waistline, just read
through the recipe . . . or perhaps skip the recipe. But be
warned that chapter 3 is devoted to Hot Brown recipes.*

THE LEGENDARY
HOT BROWN
The Real Recipe!

SERVES 2
1½ tablespoons salted butter
1½ tablespoons all-purpose flour
1½ cups heavy cream
¼ cup Pecorino Romano cheese, plus extra for garnish
Pinch of ground nutmeg
Salt and pepper
14 ounces sliced roasted turkey breast, sliced thick
4 slices of Texas toast (crusts trimmed)
4 slices of bacon
2 Roma tomatoes, sliced in half
Paprika
Parsley

In a two-quart saucepan, melt the butter and slowly whisk in flour until combined to form a thick paste or roux. Continue to cook the roux for 2 minutes over medium-low heat, stirring frequently. Whisk heavy cream into the roux and cook over medium heat until the cream begins to simmer, about 2–3 minutes. Remove sauce from heat and slowly whisk in Pecorino Romano cheese until the Mornay sauce is smooth. Add nutmeg, salt, and pepper to taste.

For each Hot Brown, place one slice of toast in an oven-safe dish and cover with 7 ounces of turkey. Take the two halves of Roma tomato and two toast points and set them alongside the base of turkey and toast. Pour half of the sauce over the dish, completely covering it. Sprinkle with additional cheese. Place entire dish under a broiler until cheese begins to brown and bubble. Remove from heat and cross two pieces of crispy bacon on top. Sprinkle with paprika and parsley and serve immediately.

THREE

Recipes

MOST READERS MIGHT BE COMPLETELY satisfied with the original Hot Brown, but there are many creative recipes by very talented chefs that used the Hot Brown as inspiration. Be warned that there are some equally horrible recipes that claim to be the same dish. This chapter will feature the great, the good, the bad, and the downright ugly! The hope is to give perspective on the Hot Brown as a historical dish and to show the variety of recipes for the Hot Brown. You can decide which one of these recipes is the best Hot Brown.

In 1949, Marion Flexner's book *Out of Kentucky Kitchens* was released to store shelves. The classic Kentucky cookbook includes a foreword from Duncan Hines—the man behind the famous name who was known for hotel and restaurant reviews. Flexner's masterpiece of a cookbook features many recipes of classic Kentucky cuisine. She included a recipe for the Hot Brown and a Cold Brown (see chapter 4). She refers to both as "The Brown Sandwich" but differentiates the two sandwiches with parentheses (cold) and (hot). Flexner also refers to the two sandwiches as "Quickie!" indicating that the sandwiches are easy and fast to prepare.

*M*ARION FLEXNER'S HOT BROWN

4 slices of toast
4 slices baked chicken or turkey (cut from the breast)
    about ¼-inch thick
¼ cup American cheese, grated
8 strips bacon, fried crisp
4 tablespoons grated Parmesan cheese
1 cup cream sauce

Blend American cheese with cream sauce until cheese has melted. Place a piece of chicken on each piece of toast, and cover with ¼ cup of sauce. Place 2 strips of bacon (previously cooked) on each sandwich, and sprinkle with 1 tablespoon of grated Parmesan cheese. Place sandwiches in a pan under the broiler until the cheese melts and becomes a golden brown. Serve at once. This recipe makes 4 portions. If you have individual shallow baking dishes, either pottery or copper, use them. This sandwich should really be served in the dish in which it was browned.

When people in Kentucky talk about "Northern Kentucky" they are speaking about that area of Kentucky just south of Cincinnati, Ohio. In fact, part of Northern Kentucky is functionally part of Cincinnati—for example, the Cincinnati International Airport is inside the state of Kentucky—but the people remain proud of their Bluegrass roots (which is why you can buy Kentucky postcards and magnets in the Cincinnati airport). In 1967, the Co-operative Society of the

Children's Hospital published *The Cincinnati Cookbook* and included a recipe for the Hot Brown. Bishop Roger Blanchard, the Episcopal bishop for Southern Ohio, wrote the foreword, and an introduction was written by Richard W. Haupt, the director of the Cincinnati Historical Society. Other Kentucky recipes are featured in the cookbook as well as many German recipes. Here is my adaptation of the *Cincinnati Cookbook*'s Hot Brown.

*N*ORTHERN KENTUCKY HOT BROWNS

SERVES 4

4 slices toast
4 slices chicken or turkey (¼-inch slices)
¼ cup grated American cheese
1 cup milk
8 strips crisp bacon
4 tablespoons grated Parmesan cheese
2 tablespoons flour
2 tablespoons butter
¼ teaspoon salt
Dash white pepper

Melt butter, blend in flour, but do not brown. Add milk gradually, stirring until smooth. Add salt and pepper. Blend American cheese with cream sauce until cheese is melted. Place sliced chicken on toast, cover with a fourth of the blended sauce. Place 2 strips of bacon on each and sprinkle with Parmesan cheese. Place in a shallow baking pan under flame until cheese melts to golden brown. Serve at once in the dish in which it has been browned. Sliced tomato can be added for variation.

J. B. Hart served under Chef Schmidt at the Brown Hotel. In a 1985 interview with the *Courier-Journal*, Hart revealed some of the history of the famous sandwich as he remembered the hotel, the chef, and the Hot Brown.[1] Perhaps this is as close to the real Hot Brown as we might get because the recipe was reported by one of Schmidt's apprentices. Please note that the recipe lacks tomatoes, and the sauce is made with milk fortified with a little cream and egg. The recipe was adapted into "family portions" by Camille Glenn. I have adapted Hart's recipe for ease of preparation.

J. B. HART'S HOT BROWN

SERVES 4 TO 6

½ stick of butter (4 tablespoons)
6 tablespoons flour
3 to 3½ cups milk
6 tablespoons grated Parmesan cheese
1 egg, beaten
1 ounce of cream, whipped
Salt, to taste
White pepper, to taste
1 to 2 pounds roast turkey, sliced
8 to 12 slices of bread, toasted and trimmed
Extra Parmesan cheese to garnish the top
8 to 12 slices of bacon, cooked

Melt the butter and add enough flour to make a reasonably thick roux, one that absorbs all the butter. Add the milk and then the Parmesan cheese, cooking until the sauce is thick. Add egg to the sauce but do not allow the sauce to boil once the egg had been added. Remove the sauce from heat, then add whipped cream, salt, and pepper.

For each Hot Brown, place 2 slices of toast in ovenproof
dishes. Cover the toast with 4 to 6 ounces of roast turkey.
Pour a generous amount of sauce over the top of the
turkey and toast. Then sprinkle with Parmesan cheese.

Place the dish under the broiler until the sauce is speckled
brown and is bubbly. Remove the dish from the broiler. Cross
two pieces of cooked bacon on top and serve immediately.

The Courier-Journal & Times Cook Book by Lillian Marshall
(1971) and *The Courier-Journal Kentucky Cookbook*, edited by
John Finley (1985), date this recipe back to 1948. The 1985
cookbook is an expanded version of the 1971 cookbook; both
include many Kentucky cuisine recipes. This recipe is complex but well worth the effort, and the recipe walks the person making the sandwiches through all the steps of making
the sandwich.

$\mathscr{L}$ILLIAN MARSHALL'S HOT BROWN SANDWICH

Simmer a hen in water seasoned with a few peppercorns,
salt, and bay leaf. When tender, cool in the broth.
After cooling, cut the breast into thin slices.

BÉCHAMEL SAUCE:
⅓ cup butter or margarine
½ medium sized sliced onion, minced
⅓ cup flour
3 cups hot milk
1 teaspoon salt

Dash of red pepper
Sprigs of parsley
Dash of nutmeg

Melt the butter or margarine in a saucepan. Add onion and cook slowly until light brown, about 15 or 20 minutes. Add flour and blend until the flour makes a smooth paste with the onion minces in it. Add milk and other seasonings and cook, stirring constantly and briskly, until the sauce is thick and smooth. Then continue to cook, stirring occasionally, about 25 minutes altogether. Strain. If the sauce isn't to be used immediately, stir occasionally to keep a crust from forming on the top.

ORNAY SAUCE

2 cups Béchamel sauce
2 egg yolks
½ cup Parmesan cheese, grated
1 tablespoon butter or margarine
4 tablespoons whipped cream

Heat the Béchamel sauce and combine with egg yolks. Stir constantly and remove from heat as soon as it starts to boil. When hot and thick, add cheese and the butter or margarine. The sauce must not boil or it will curdle.

Then, for every ½ cup sauce that is to be used for the sandwich, fold in 1 tablespoon of whipped cream. Here it would be 4 tablespoons. Fry as many strips of bacon as the number of sandwiches you are fixing. Sauté a mushroom cap for each sandwich.

To assemble, cut the crusts off 2 slices of bread for each sandwich and toast them. Put 1 slice of toast in an ovenproof shallow dish. Lay the slices of chicken on top of the toast. Cover with a heaping portion of the sauce. Place in a very hot oven or under the broiler until the sauce takes on the glow of a suntan. Cut the extra slice of toast diagonally, and put the tips at each end. Top with bacon strip and the mushroom.

A little more grated cheese mixed with bread crumbs can be sprinkled over the sauce.

Volume 2 of *Prescriptions for Cooks*, which was compiled by the Women's Auxiliary to the Jefferson County Medical Society in 1971 includes a chapter titled "Lagniappe." Lagniappe is a Creole word for "a little something extra," such as the thirteenth roll, muffin, or donut in a "baker's dozen." I have always enjoyed the fact that Louisville and New Orleans shared French in their heritage, cooking, and attitudes. I am glad to have enjoyed living in both of these cities.

$\mathscr{H}$ OT BROWN— IMPERIAL HOUSE

SERVES 4

12 ounces sliced white meat of turkey

4 ounces thinly sliced baked Kentucky ham

8 slices of bacon, ⅔ done

4 slices of toast, cut diagonally

8 slices tomato (optional)

2 tablespoons grated Parmesan cheese

Paprika

SAUCE:
1 quart milk
½ cup butter
½ cup plus 2 tablespoons flour
1 teaspoon salt
½ cup grated Parmesan cheese

Place milk in a two-quart saucepan and bring to nearly the boiling point. In a separate four-quart saucepan, melt butter until clarified. Add flour and blend until flour is a blond color. Remove both pans from heat and gradually pour milk into butter, beating with a wire whip until sauce is mixed well. Return sauce to heat and continue stirring until it begins to thicken. Add salt and ½ cup Parmesan cheese; cook 2 minutes or more until cheese melts and blends with sauce.

To assemble: place 2 half slices of toast for each person in individual shallow casserole. Over the toast, arrange slices of turkey and country ham; cover well with sauce. Top with 2 slices of tomato (optional) and bacon. Sprinkle with 2 tablespoons Parmesan cheese and paprika. Place in 400° oven until sauce becomes bubbly and the fat of the bacon melts over the sauce. (This can be done in one large casserole instead of in individual ones.)

Louisville has many official sister cities—Montpellier, France (1954), Quito, Ecuador (1962), Tamale, Ghana (1979), Mainz, Germany (1994), La Plata, Argentina (1994), Perm, Russia (1994), Jiujiang, PR China (2004), Leeds, England (2006), and Adapazari, Turkey (2012)—but one must also consider New Orleans an unofficial sister city of Louisville because of the long-held association between the two cities.[2] After

Hurricane Katrina, many New Orleans residents relocated to Louisville while the city recovered, and some of them stayed. May Ball of the First Presbyterian Church in New Orleans proves this close association with her contribution of a recipe for Hot Browns to *More Favorites from First*, a cookbook produced by the church. The following is a recipe based on May Ball's recipe for Hot Browns.

$\mathscr{H}$OT BROWNS

SERVES 4

6 tablespoons butter

6 tablespoons flour

½ teaspoon salt

¼ teaspoon pepper

1½ cups milk

½ teaspoon Worcestershire sauce

¾ cup cheddar cheese, grated

Cheddar or Parmesan cheese for topping

8 button mushrooms, sliced and sautéed in butter
    (optional)

⅛ cup frozen peas, cooked (optional)

4 slices of toast

12 slices of turkey or chicken

8 slices of bacon, cooked

To make cheese sauce, melt butter in small skillet. Whisk in the flour, salt, and pepper until there are no lumps. Whisk in the milk, then add the Worcestershire, ¾ cup of the cheese, mushrooms, and peas. Cook until the cheese melts and the sauce thickens, adding more milk if necessary.

To assemble the dish, lay slices of toast in the bottom of four individual casseroles. Put slices of chicken or turkey next, then the bacon. Pour cheese sauce over all and sprinkle a little additional grated cheese on top. Put in a hot oven (400°) for about 20 minutes or under the broiler until the top is brown and the sauce bubbles. The sauce can be made ahead and frozen, but reheat well before pouring over the meat.

The Harvey Browne Memorial Presbyterian Church in St. Matthews, Kentucky (now part of metropolitan Louisville) has enjoyed over one hundred years of worship and serving the community. In 1984, the church brought all their recipes together to form a new cookbook which they named *Hot Browne*. The fourth recipe in the book is for a "Hot Browne" that was contributed by Billye Eblen. The following recipe is based on the recipe featured in the cookbook.

HE HOT BROWNE

SERVES 4

SAUCE:

6 tablespoons butter

6 tablespoons flour

1½ cups milk

¼ teaspoon onion salt

Few dashes of black pepper

1½ teaspoons seasoned chicken stock

¾ cup shredded cheddar cheese

4 slices bacon, fried crisp

Sliced cooked chicken or turkey (white meat is best!)

        Parmesan cheese, grated
        Paprika
        4 slices of bread, toasted
        4 halves of peaches or 8 slices of tomato

*Melt the butter, add the flour, and stir until the mixture
is smooth and thick. Make sure that very little color is
added to the mixture. Slowly add the milk, then add the
other ingredients. Cook until smooth and thick, stirring
until mixture almost reaches boiling point, but don't allow
the sauce to boil! Remove the sauce from the heat.*

To assemble the sandwiches:

*On four ovenproof plates or a bread pan, arrange
the toast slices. Place chicken or turkey on the bread
and cover with sauce, then add bacon. Sprinkle with
Parmesan cheese and paprika. Place under broiler until
sauce begins to bubble and starts to tan. Garnish with
the peach halves or the tomato slices. Serve at once.*

Hot Browns are so delicious that some people might want to
go back for a second helping! The Harvey Browne Memorial
Presbyterian Church's first cookbook was so popular that a
second was published in 2003, named: *Hot Browne: A Second
Helping.* Of course, the book includes a "Hot Browne," in this
case, a Louisville Hot Browne. This recipe is more complex
than the one listed in the *Hot Browne* from 1984. Here is the
adapted recipe from this book.

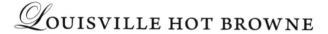 $\mathcal{L}$OUISVILLE HOT BROWNE

4 tablespoons butter
1 small onion, chopped
3 tablespoons flour
2 cups milk
½ teaspoon salt
¼ teaspoon white pepper
¼ cup shredded cheddar cheese
¼ cup Parmesan cheese, grated
8 slices toast, crust removed
Slices of cooked turkey or chicken breast
8 crisply fried bacon slices
8 slices tomato

Melt the butter in a pan or pot. Add onions and sauté until translucent, then add the flour and combine. Add milk, salt, and pepper and whisk until smooth. Make sure to stir the combination frequently. Cook on medium heat until sauce thickens. Add cheeses and continue heating until they blend. Remove from heat. Put 1 slice of toast in each of four ovenproof individual serving dishes. Cut the remaining toast slices diagonally and place on the sides of sandwiches. Top each slice of toast with slices of turkey or chicken. Ladle cheese sauce over the sandwiches. Place under the broiler until the sauce begins to bubble. Garnish with bacon and tomato and serve immediately.

How to Boil Water, by Betty Jane Donahoe, is a classic Kentucky cookbook from 1972. The premise behind the book was to teach young women a group of recipes that they might cook for their husbands. The premise might be out of touch with the values of today's young professionals but the recipes are still good. This cookbook starts with simple fare, with a chapter on hamburgers and another on hot dogs. There are several hints in the regional recipes that this is a Kentucky cookbook; one is the Hot Brown. This recipe is based on the Hot Brown in this book.

$\mathcal{B}$ETTY JANE DONAHOE'S HOT BROWN

Enough sliced chicken for 4 sandwiches
8 strips of bacon
5 cups of grated cheddar cheese
4 pieces of toast
6 tablespoons butter
6 tablespoons flour
2 cups milk
1 cup chicken bouillon (2 cubes, dissolved)
½ teaspoon salt
½ teaspoon pepper

Slice enough chicken or turkey for four sandwiches. Fry bacon and set aside. Toast 4 pieces of bread and set aside. Now the following takes a little doing. You must be careful when you combine the flour and butter. This must be done over a low heat and the flour must be added slowly, while stirring all the while. Should you scorch the flour, toss it out and start over. After the flour has been combined with the butter, add the milk slowly and continuously. Next add the dissolved chicken bouillon slowly and continue stirring. Add the grated cheese and slowly stir until the cheese has melted. When the cheese has melted you should have a rich and creamy cheese sauce. Add the salt and pepper and stir some more.

*Cover each piece of toast with chicken or turkey and
spoon the cheese sauce all over. Garnish each with
two pieces of bacon and serve immediately.*

Colonel Sanders and his famous Kentucky Fried Chicken
with the secret recipe containing eleven herbs and spices is
known around the world. However, many people did not realize that his wife Claudia had a dinner house in Shelbyville. In
1979, *The Claudia Sanders Dinner House of Shelbyville, Kentucky,
Cookbook* was authored by Cherry Settle, Tommy Settle, and
Edward G. Klemm Jr., and proved that the eleven herbs and
spices is not the only special ingredient used by the Sanders
family. For the Hot Brown, they substitute canned peaches
for tomatoes. This recipe is based on the one in the Sanders
cookbook.

$\mathscr{C}$LAUDIA SANDERS'S DINNER HOUSE HOT BROWN

SERVES 1

1½ cups cheese sauce (see below)
1 slice white toast
1 slice white turkey meat
1 slice Claudia Sanders Kentucky Country Ham
2 slices of bacon
¼ cup grated sharp cheese
¼ cup grated Parmesan cheese
1 peach half (canned)
Paprika, to garnish

1. *Preheat oven to 400°.*
2. *Put 2 tablespoons cheese sauce on bottom of an individual baking dish.*
3. *Place the toast on this sauce.*
4. *Cover the toast with 3 tablespoons cheese sauce.*
5. *Put layer of ham over this.*
6. *Cover with 3 tablespoons cheese sauce.*
7. *Sprinkle half of the Parmesan cheese on this layer of cheese sauce and add the slice of turkey.*
8. *Cover with 3 tablespoons cheese sauce.*
9. *Sprinkle the grated sharp cheese over this.*
10. *Sprinkle on the rest of the Parmesan cheese, and place peach half in center of the sandwich.*
11. *Garnish with paprika.*
12. *Place 1 slice of bacon at each side of the peach half.*
13. *Bake at 400° for 15 minutes.*
14. *Serve in baking dish while hot.*

Claudia Sanders's Cheese Sauce for Hot Brown

Yield: 1½ cups sauce (enough for 1 sandwich)
2 tablespoons margarine
2 tablespoons all-purpose flour
1 cup milk
1 cup shredded cheddar cheese
¼ teaspoon salt
Dash of white pepper

1. *Melt margarine in saucepan over low heat.*
2. *Blend in the flour, salt, and white pepper.*
3. *Add milk slowly, stirring as you add it.*
4. *Put in the shredded cheese and continue to cook and stir until the cheese has completely melted.*

Charles Patteson is a native Kentuckian who lived in New York where he owned both a public relations firm and a catering company, the Festive Food Company. In 1988, he wrote *Charles Patteson's Kentucky Cooking*. In his cookbook, Patteson includes a description of "Louisville's two Grand Hotels," the Brown Hotel and the Seelbach Hotel, as well as other hotels and inns that are still famous more than thirty years later, such as the Beaumont Inn and the Science Hill Inn. He included a recipe for the Hot Brown and the Brown Hotel's Chicken Chow Mein (see chapter 4), which was very famous at one time, and more than one hundred other recipes related to Kentucky cuisine. Patteson mentioned that the recipe he included was "graciously given us for reproduction here," even though this recipe does not look like the recipe that the Brown uses today.

CHARLES PATTESON'S HOT BROWN

SERVES 2

6 tablespoons butter

½ cup plus 2 tablespoons all-purpose flour

1½ cups half-and-half

1½ cups heavy cream

⅓ cup grated Romano cheese

⅓ cup grated Parmesan cheese

½ cup sweet sherry, boiled for 1 minute

2 egg yolks, beaten

4 toast points

½ pound turkey breast slices

4 tomato wedges

4 strips crisp cooked bacon

Parsley

In a heavy saucepan, melt the butter. Sprinkle on the flour and stir constantly until the roux is golden brown and dry.

Stir in the half-and-half and the cream. Cook several minutes, or until the flour taste is gone. Stir in the Romano and Parmesan cheeses. Add the sherry and continue stirring until the sauce is thin and the cheese is melted.

Strain the hot sauce into a bowl. Add the egg yolk and blend well. The sauce may be reheated, but do not boil.

Preheat the broiler. Line 2 ovenproof, single serving dishes with 2 toast points. Top with slices of turkey and a generous covering of sauce. Broil until the sauce is lightly browned on top.

Remove and place 2 tomato wedges and 2 bacon strips crisscrossed, on each sandwich. Garnish with parsley. Serve hot.

The "authentic" Hot Brown recipe has been featured in many cookbooks and articles: locally, regionally, nationally, and even internationally. This recipe was listed as the "original" Hot Brown sandwich in the 1992 book, *Dining in Historic Kentucky*, by Marty Godbey. This recipe is a little on the "light" side compared to the recipe for the Hot Brown used by the Brown Hotel today, but it is still a very good recipe and is like the recipe from J. B. Hart.

$\mathscr{T}$HE "AUTHENTIC"
HOT BROWN *from the Brown Hotel*

SERVES 6

4 ounces of butter

6 tablespoons of flour

3 to 3½ cups of milk

6 tablespoons grated Parmesan cheese

1 egg, beaten

1 ounce heavy cream, whipped

Salt, to taste

Pepper, to taste

Sliced roasted turkey breast

12 slices toast

Grated Parmesan cheese

12 strips of bacon

In a skillet, melt the butter; add flour and stir until absorbed. Stir in milk and cheese; add egg. Do not allow to boil. Remove from heat and fold in cream with seasonings. For each Hot Brown, place 2 slices toast on ovenproof dish. Cover with turkey and sauce. Sprinkle with additional cheese and broil until speckled brown and bubbling. Remove from broiler, cross two strips of cooked bacon on top, and serve at once.

David Dominé, author of *Adventures in New Kentucky Cooking* (2007), brilliantly liquefies the Hot Brown into a soup. Dominé, the self-described Bluegrass Peasant, is the author of many books, including cookbooks and books related to ghost stories in Louisville. The recipe is also found in *Derby Entertaining: Traditional Kentucky Recipes*.[3] This is a riff on Dominé's original recipe.

DAVID DOMINÉ'S HOT BROWN SOUP

8 strips of Kentucky bacon

1 cup finely chopped onion

½ cup finely chopped celery

4 large cloves of garlic, minced

2 medium red potatoes, peeled and cut in ¼-inch pieces

3 cups diced turkey breast

2 cups dry white wine

2 cups chicken stock

5 cups milk

2 teaspoons kosher salt

1 teaspoon ground white pepper

¼ teaspoon ground nutmeg

2 cups heavy cream

½ cup all-purpose flour

2 cups shredded aged white cheddar cheese

Homemade croutons—made by cubing bread and lightly toasting in the oven.

Crumbled bacon, chopped tomato, croutons, and chopped fresh parsley for garnish

In a Dutch oven or large pot, cook bacon over medium heat until slightly crispy. Add onion, celery, and garlic and sauté until tender. Add diced potatoes and turkey and cook, stirring occasionally, until turkey is seared on all sides. Add the wine. Turn up the heat and stir to deglaze the bottom of the pan. Cook for 5 minutes and then add the stock, milk, salt, pepper, and nutmeg. Simmer over low heat for 15 minutes, or until the potatoes are tender, stirring often to avoid sticking on the bottom. In a small bowl, whisk together cream and flour to make a slurry free of lumps and stir into the simmering soup. After the mixture has thickened, turn off the heat, add cheese and stir. Adjust the seasoning if necessary and serve with desired toppings.

Dominé explores another version of the Hot Brown with this tart in his book, *Splash of Bourbon Kentucky's Spirit*. This book explores many recipes; each features bourbon. His book was released in 2010 about the same time as my book, *The Kentucky Bourbon Cookbook*. Between the two books a cook will have many recipes that feature America's original spirit and Kentucky's favorite! Here is my adaptation on Dominé's Hot Brown tart.

$\mathscr{H}$OT BROWN TART À LA DOMINÉ

Pastry dough for a 12-inch cast iron skillet
6 large eggs
1 cup heavy cream
¼ cup bourbon
½ teaspoon kosher salt
¼ teaspoon ground white pepper
1 cup chopped cooked turkey breast
1 cup grated white extra-sharp cheddar cheese
8 slices cooked (not too crispy) bacon, chopped
2 small tomatoes, thinly sliced
¼ cup grated Parmesan cheese

Preheat the oven to 350° and line the skillet with the pastry dough. Beat the eggs with the cream, bourbon, salt and pepper.

*Place turkey breast on tart crust, and top with cheddar cheese
and bacon. Pour the egg mixture over the cheese, and layer
tomatoes over the top. Sprinkle with the Parmesan cheese
and bake for 30 minutes or until a knife inserted in the middle
comes out clean. The top should be brown and crusty. Remove
from the oven, let sit for 5 minutes and serve piping hot.*

Sarah Fritschner was a food writer and critic for the Louisville *Courier-Journal* for many years. She is also the author
of many books, including *Sarah Fritschner's Holidays: Menus
and Recipes for the Fall Holiday Season*, which was published in
2004. In this recipe, Fritschner moves the Hot Brown from an
individual dish to one that serves a family. She also simplifies
that production and serving of the Hot Brown so that most
people will be able to make a Hot Brown casserole with ease.
This is my interpretation of Fritschner's original recipe.

$\mathscr{S}$ARAH FRITSCHNER'S
HOT BROWN CASSEROLE

SERVES 6

2 cups toasted bread cubes, from Texas toast

2 cups diced, cooked turkey breast

SAUCE:

½ cup butter

⅔ cup flour

1 teaspoon salt

1 teaspoon (freshly ground) black pepper

4 cups milk (low-fat will work)

3 cups shredded sharp cheddar cheese

TOPPING:
½ cup shredded Parmesan cheese
6 slices bacon, cooked then crumbled
1 cup diced tomatoes or cut-up cherry tomatoes

Heat oven to 350°. Place bread cubes in the bottom of a 2-quart casserole. Top with diced turkey. Set aside.

To make the sauce: Melt butter in a medium sized pan. Add flour, salt, and pepper and stir to blend. Slowly whisk in milk. The mixture will be thick and hard to stir at first; just stir the milk in little by little until it loosens up, then add the rest of the milk all at once. Continue to cook, and stir until mixture bubbles. Remove from heat and add cheddar cheese. Stir until melted and the mixture is smooth. Pour sauce over bread and turkey. Sprinkle with Parmesan cheese, then with bacon and tomato bits. Bake 20 to 25 minutes, or until the casserole is hot and bubbly.

One of the stories related to the creation of the Hot Brown suggests a customer consumed too much alcohol, and that the sandwich was created to help with the effects of the alcohol. If you are in the mood for the flavor of a Hot Brown early in the morning you might try this recipe for the Benedict Brown. This recipe is the product of a melding of the Hot Brown with Eggs Benedict.

ENEDICT BROWN

8 eggs
Butter
4 English muffins

8 slices of Canadian bacon
8 slices of turkey breast
2 tomatoes, cut into 8 wedges each
8 slices bacon
Parmesan cheese to garnish
2 cups Mornay sauce (see below)

Poach the eggs in simmering water into which a teaspoon of white vinegar has been added. Split and toast the English muffin, then add butter. Fry the Canadian bacon and turkey breast. Place the Canadian bacon and turkey on the English muffin, bacon slices on top of the turkey, and poached egg on top of the bacon slices. Cover with Mornay sauce. Garnish with wedges of tomato and Parmesan cheese. Serve.

MORNAY SAUCE:
4 tablespoons butter
3 tablespoons flour
¼ cup red onion, julienned
2 cups milk
Salt
White pepper
4 ounces of Swiss cheese
1 ounce of Parmesan cheese

In a pan, over warm heat, add the butter and melt. Once the butter is melted, add the flour and stir the two together. Cook together for a few minutes, then cool the resulting roux. In a small saucepan, heat the milk and red onion together until boiling. Take off the burner and strain milk to remove onion. Return the milk to the saucepan, add the cool roux, and stir briskly. Once the sauce thickens, add salt and white pepper to taste. Add the two cheeses and stir until incorporated. Serve.

When I moved to North Carolina I discovered that most *everything* here is served on a biscuit or with a biscuit—in fact we have restaurant chains that specialize in serving gravy, ham, sausage, chicken, pork tenderloins, chicken fried steak, not to mention eggs and cheese and even pimento cheese on biscuits—which is a good thing because I love biscuits! The next time I made Hot Browns I tried substituting biscuits for bread because Mornay sauce is basically cheese gravy! Biscuits are the perfect bread for a version of the Hot Brown and make a tasty treat. The biscuit recipe below is like the baking powdered biscuit recipe found in *Cabbage Patch: Famous Kentucky Recipes* (1956). The *Cabbage Patch* cookbook is an amazing book with many recipes, including "Chow Mein, Manderin (*sic*) Style as served at the Brown Hotel," but one recipe that the cookbook does not include is one for a Hot Brown.

$\mathcal{C}$AROLINA BROWN

SERVES BETWEEN 1 AND 2
    depending on how much you like to eat!
First make the biscuits. . .
2 cups of flour
4 teaspoons baking powder
1 teaspoon salt
6 tablespoons lard
⅔ cup milk

Mix the dry ingredients; sift twice. Cut in the lard, then add the milk, mixing to a soft dough. Place the dough on a floured board. Roll lightly to ½-inch thickness. Shape with a biscuit cutter. Place on a buttered pan and brush the top with melted butter. Bake at 450° for 12 to 15 minutes.

2 large biscuits, split open
4 ounces, turkey, sliced
4 tomato wedges
4 ounces sharp cheddar cheese, grated
4 strips bacon, cooked
½ ounce Parmesan cheese, grated
6 ounces crème or Béchamel sauce

Preheat the broiler on your oven to 400°. Arrange the biscuits in a baking dish. Toast the biscuits under the broiler until a little crispy. Warm the crème sauce on the stove, then add the sharp cheddar cheese and continue to warm until the cheese is melted. You now have a cheddar Mornay sauce. Place the turkey on top of the biscuits. Warm in the oven until the turkey is warmed through, then pull the baking dish from the oven. Pour the warm Mornay sauce over the top of the biscuits. Add the bacon to the top of the biscuits in a cross pattern. Place the tomato wedges in the areas between the bacon and top with Parmesan cheese. Place the baking dish under the broiler again until the Parmesan cheese browns lightly.

Robert "Bobby" William Flay is a celebrity chef and the owner of a restaurant empire. He is a graduate of the French Culinary Institute (now the International Culinary Center) in New York City. Chef Flay conducted a Hot Brown throwdown with Chef Joe Castro and Chef John Castro in 2008. The Brothers Castro won the day with their traditional Hot Brown, but Chef Flay had a close second with a French Toast Hot Brown. Here is my version based on Flay's recipe. I am calling this recipe the Bobby Brown in honor of Chef Flay's contribution to this classic sandwich.

OBBY BROWN

SERVES 1

2 slices of Texas toast
2 large eggs
¼ cup milk
2 tablespoons butter
Salt, to taste
Pepper, to taste
4 ounces turkey, sliced
2 tomato slices, grilled
3 ounces sharp cheddar cheese, grated
2 strips bacon, cooked
½ ounce Parmesan cheese, grated
4 ounces crème or Béchamel sauce

Mix the egg and milk until completely incorporated. Add salt and pepper to taste. Dip the Texas toast into the egg and milk mixture and allow the bread to soak up the liquid. Heat a pan on the stove and melt butter. Add the batter-soaked bread to the pan and cook on one side, then flip and cook on the other side until completely cooked. Cut one of the pieces of French toast in half diagonally. Preheat the broiler on your oven to 400°. Arrange the French toast in a baking dish. Warm the crème or Béchamel sauce on the stove then add the sharp cheddar cheese and Parmesan cheese. Continue to warm until the cheese is melted. You now have a Mornay sauce. Place the turkey on top of the French toast. Warm in the oven until the turkey is warmed through, then pull the baking dish from the oven. Pour the warm Mornay sauce over the top of the turkey and French toast. Add the bacon to the top of the Mornay sauce in a cross pattern. Grill the tomato slices and slice them in half. Place the tomato

slices in the areas between the bacon. Place the baking dish
under the broiler again until the sandwich is warm and bubbly.

I worked with Chef Sam Mudd at Sullivan University's NCHS for sixteen years. Chef Mudd spent his whole career in Louisville—almost fifty years! Once he told me that he watched Neil Armstrong walk on the moon in 1969 while working at his first job at the Ponderosa Steak House. Chef Mudd worked many places in Louisville, including the Galt House, the Colonel Sanders Inn (which is now a Sullivan University student residence hall: Gardiner Point), the Executive West Hotel (now the Crowne Plaza), the Hunting Creek Country Club in Prospect, and others, before joining the NCHS. Chef Mudd has a profound sense of humor and a very professional demeanor, which means he was always a joy to work with in the classroom and lab. We worked closely on several ice-carving projects and on teaching basic skills. One of the remarkable things about the food service industry is learning from colleagues. One of the recipes I learned from Chef Mudd is the Hot Brown appetizer. "The big platter (of hot brown) is too much," said Chef Mudd, "but the small passed one was perfect." Other small versions include the Hot Brown tartlet at the Brown Hotel for weddings and receptions. Chef Mudd learned an appetizer like this one from Clements Catering, which is the first group he ever saw do something like this. "We served a lot of them," he also added, "I worked there for nine years and never got tired of these little hot browns." This is a perfect starter for a Derby Party or your next dinner party. "This one is a winner," explained Chef Mudd, "because you can do the prep ahead of time, they are tasty, and because they are filling."

 OT BROWN APPETIZER

24 SMALL SERVINGS
12 miniature bagels, split in half for 24 bite-size morsels
2 cups crème sauce or béchamel sauce
24 ounces turkey, sliced
2 tomatoes, diced
12 strips bacon, cooked and diced
2 bunches green onion, chopped
12 ounces Parmesan cheese, grated
6 ounces cheddar cheese, grated

Arrange the bagel halves on a sheet pan lined with aluminum foil. Warm the crème sauce or béchamel sauce on the stove then add half the parmesan cheese and continue to warm until the cheese is melted. You now have Mornay sauce. Place the turkey on top of the bagels. Pour a dollop of the warm Mornay sauce over the top of the turkey on the bagel. Top with the other half of the Parmesan cheese and the cheddar cheese. Warm in the oven until the turkey is warmed through, then pull the sheet pan from the oven. Sprinkle the diced tomato, bacon, and green onions over the bagels. Place the sheet pan under the broiler again briefly to warm and then serve immediately.

If you like your salads cold, perhaps you should try this "ode to the Hot Brown," which first appeared in David Dominé's cookbook, *Splash of Bourbon: Kentucky's Spirit.*

HE COLD BROWN SALAD
with Bourbon Buttermilk Dressing

---

1 head iceberg lettuce
1 cup buttermilk
1 cup mayonnaise
3 tablespoons apple cider vinegar
3 tablespoons bourbon
½ teaspoon kosher salt
¼ teaspoon ground white pepper
2 large tomatoes, sliced
1 small turkey breast, cooked and chopped (about
    2 cups)
6–8 slices of bacon, broken in half
Asiago cheese, grated
Toast points

Wash the lettuce and cut into 6–8 wedges. Prepare the dressing by whisking together the buttermilk, mayonnaise, vinegar, bourbon, salt, and pepper. Assemble individual salads by laying several slices of tomato over each wedge of lettuce and drizzling with buttermilk dressing. Top with chopped turkey and bacon. Garnish with slivers of Asiago cheese and toast points.

After high school graduation, I moved to Lincoln, Nebraska, to attend college. One of the culinary pleasures that I experienced in Nebraska was the Runza. Runza is a fast-food restaurant that bears the name of the signature sandwich, which is the trademarked name for a "bierock," or seasoned ground meat, cabbage, and onion encased in bread. One of the benefits of eating a Runza is that this sandwich is portable;

they are easy to eat on the run—perfect for a college student! During my college years, I worked as a baker for the Miller & Payne Department store downtown; we made some amazing cinnamon rolls and cookies. That was a long time ago. Miller & Payne closed when many department stores closed and homogenized into Dillard's and Macy's. In 2006, Runza acquired the recipe and method for making the Miller & Payne cinnamon rolls. So even though the original store has closed down, the cinnamon rolls I used to make are still available! This next Hot Brown recipe is inspired by the Runza, but in this case, the turkey, bacon, tomatoes, and cheese sauce are enclosed in bread.

$\mathcal{P}$ORTABLE HOT BROWN

2 packages of active dry yeast

¾ cup and 1 tablespoon sugar

1 cup water

1 tablespoon salt

2 cups warm milk

8 cups flour

½ cup lard

2 eggs

1 pound turkey breast, cooked and diced small

6 ounces bacon, cooked and crumbled

6 ounces Parmesan cheese, grated

2 tomatoes, diced small

1 cup Mornay sauce (see pp. 8, 10)

Salt, to taste

Pepper, to taste

*For the dough, use a large mixing bowl or the bowl on a
KitchenAid mixer. Start by mixing the yeast, tablespoon of
sugar, and water. Allow this mixture to proof. Add the milk,
eggs, salt, and ¾ cup sugar, and mix together. In a separate
large bowl, cut the lard into 4 cups flour until it resembles
cornmeal, then add to the mixing bowl with the liquid mixture
and mix together. Let this mixture rise. After this mixture
has risen, add the other 4 cups of flour, one cup at a time, and
mix until you have a smooth dough; then let the dough rise
again. While it rises, mix the turkey, bacon, cheese, tomato,
and cream sauce together into a uniform mixture. Season
with salt and pepper. Preheat oven to 350°. Once the dough
has risen, punch it down and cut into 20 pieces. Roll out
the pieces of dough, spoon filling onto each piece, and wrap
them up. Bake for about 15 minutes on greased sheets.*

Another portable option for the Hot Brown is a Hot Brown
Wrap. This sandwich can be consumed hot or cold. For the
sauce, we are substituting a mayonnaise-based sauce that
will add creaminess and a little acid for balance in the sandwich. This sandwich is easier and quicker to put together
than the previous recipe, so it is perfect for people on the go
with little time.

ℋOT BROWN WRAP

SERVES 2

2 large flour tortillas, 12- or 14-inch

8 ounces sliced roasted turkey breast

4 strips of bacon

1 tomato sliced into thin wedges

½ cup of Parmesan cheese, grated
½ cup mayonnaise
2 tablespoons white wine vinegar
Salt, to taste
Pepper, to taste

Prepare all the ingredients. Then make the dressing by adding the mayonnaise, Parmesan cheese, and vinegar together and mix. Season the dressing with salt and pepper. Warm all of the ingredients so they are hot and ready to go into the sandwich. In a warm skillet, heat the flour tortillas on each side. As you pull a tortilla out of the skillet, spread dressing on it. Then fill the tortilla with the warm turkey, 2 slices of bacon, and slices of tomato. Wrap the tortilla up folding the ends in and then rolling the sandwich up.

Chef Ouita Michel has been nominated for multiple James Beard awards. So, it is not a surprise that when celebrity chef Guy Fieri traveled the country seeking out great eats on his show, *Diners, Drive-ins and Dives*, he would include one of Chef Michel's properties and one of her dishes. Wallace Station, in Versailles, Kentucky (pronounced VER-sales for those outside of the Bluegrass), features two dishes that are inspired by the Hot Brown, the "Big Brown Burger," which Chef Fieri named one of his top five burgers, and the "Inside Out Hot Brown." The Inside Out Hot Brown is a grilled sandwich that includes all of the elements of a Hot Brown but in a traditional sandwich. The following is my interpretation of Chef Michel's Big Brown Burger.

THE BIG BROWN BURGER

SERVES 4

4 large hamburger buns

2 pounds 85 percent ground beef

4 1-ounce slices of ham, warmed

1 cup Mornay sauce (with white cheddar cheese,
    see pp. 8, 10)

1 tomato, sliced

8 slices of bacon, cooked

¼ cup Worcestershire sauce

Salt, to taste

Pepper, to taste

Butter for the buns

Lay out all of the ingredients. Mix the Worcestershire sauce, salt, and pepper into the hamburger meat; then make four 8-ounce patties. Grill the hamburgers until desired doneness. Lightly butter the buns and brown both sides in a skillet. Once the buns are finished, place the patties on top of the buns, the warmed ham on top of each of the patties, 2 ounces of Mornay sauce on each patty, then top with 2 pieces of bacon each. Serve at once.

If you love hash as much as I do you might try making this hash with leftovers from Thanksgiving. The hash makes a good dinner or a nice accompaniment for breakfast the next morning. Serve with eggs, or just eat the hash.

HOT BROWN HASH

SERVES 6
2 tablespoons butter
1 small onion
2 medium potatoes, peeled and cut into small cubes
4 cups cooked turkey, shredded
6 slices bacon, cooked and chopped
1 tomato, diced
1 teaspoon salt
½ teaspoon pepper
2 cups Mornay sauce
Parmesan cheese, grated

In a skillet, melt the butter and cook the onion until tender; add the potatoes with enough water to cover, then simmer until the potatoes are tender, about 20 minutes. Add the turkey, bacon, tomato, salt, and pepper, and simmer for another 30 minutes. Top with Mornay sauce, a fried or poached egg, and Parmesan cheese.

I love pasta! One of my favorite pasta dishes is the carbonara. The story goes that carbonara was created as a hearty meal for coal miners or coal workers. The dish would sustain them during their long, grueling day of work. Kentucky is still the third largest producer of coal in the United States, which means there are still many coal miners in Kentucky. Carbonara already has several components—bacon, cheese, and bread (in the form of pasta)—of the Hot Brown. This next recipe is basically a carbonara with the addition of turkey and tomatoes. Don't be fooled! This is not only a dish for coal

miners, but for anyone who likes a Hot Brown. In fact, enjoy
one before a long, exhausting day at the track!

ASTA BROWN

SERVES 4
12 ounces pappardelle or fettuccine
¼ cup plus 2 tablespoons olive oil
2 medium shallots, finely chopped
Kosher salt, to taste
Finely ground black pepper, to taste
4 ounces pancetta, sliced in small pieces
8 ounces turkey breast, sliced in small pieces
¾ cup Pecorino Romano cheese, grated
¾ cup Parmigiano-Reggiano cheese, grated
½ cup heavy cream
3 egg yolks
10 cherry tomatoes, cut in half

*Start by cutting the pancetta and turkey into pieces; a small
dice is an appropriate size for this dish. On the stove, set up a
pot with water and salt, and bring it to a boil. Cook the pasta
until it is al dente and drain it, reserving 1 cup of water. As
the pasta is cooking, heat the olive oil in a large skillet over a
medium-high heat. When the oil is hot, add the pancetta and
shallots, then cook for about 10 minutes over a low flame until
the pancetta has rendered most of its fat but is still chewy and
barely browned. Then add the turkey and cook until warm.
Pull the two meats and shallots off the heat and set aside. In
a bowl, slowly whisk about ½ cup of the pasta water into the
egg yolks, then add the cream and mix. Add the grated cheese
and mix thoroughly with a fork. Transfer pasta to the skillet*

with the turkey and pancetta. Toss it and turn off the heat.
Add the cream, egg, and cheese mixture to the pasta while
stirring in the remaining pasta water to help thin the sauce.
Add the pepper, and toss all the ingredients to coat the pasta.

If you feel like adding a little flair to your Hot Brown and adding a little spice to go along with the heat, try a Marron Caliente. These taco-style Hot Browns are perfect as a nice twist for your next Derby party or for something different the day after Thanksgiving. Enjoy!

MARRÓN CALIENTE
South of the Border Hot Brown

SERVES 4

8 flour taco shells

1 pound turkey breast, shredded

8 slices of bacon, cooked

1 cup *pico de gallo* (see recipe below)

1 cup Queso Fresco Mornay sauce (pp. 8, 10)

Parmesan cheese

Heat the shredded turkey. Then heat the flour tortillas.
Drizzle the sauce across the tortilla. Add the slice
of bacon. Top with shredded turkey, *pico de gallo* and
Parmesan cheese. Serve while hot!

Pico de Gallo

1 tomato, diced

1 onion, diced

1 jalapeno, seeded and diced

1 bunch of cilantro

1 green onion, chopped

½ teaspoon garlic powder
Salt, to taste
Pepper, to taste

Mix all the ingredients together so they are evenly blended. Allow the ingredients to stand together in the refrigerator for at least 30 minutes so that the flavors meld.

I feel fortunate to have lived in both Louisville and New Orleans and have strong connections to both cities. Between them, I have experienced many gastronomic firsts: my first raw oyster, my first taste of beer, my first taste of bourbon, my first muffuletta, my first po'boy sandwich and my first Hot Brown. In elementary school, I enjoyed my first crepe. Something I like about crepes is they work equally well in savory or sweet dishes. Here I have combined the idea of a Hot Brown and stuffed crepes, which celebrates the French heritage of both cities.

HE LOUIS (LOU-EE) BROWN

SERVES 8

First make crepes. Then make the Mornay sauce. Make the filling. Stuff the crepes. Cover with sauce. Top with cooked bacon and cheese. Bake. Garnish with tomatoes. Eat!

HOMEMADE CREPES:
4 eggs plus 1 egg yolk
1½ cups flour
1½ cups milk
2 tablespoons butter, melted
Dash of salt

*Beat the eggs, egg yolk, and salt together. Add the flour
and the milk alternately and keep beating until smooth.
Add the melted butter and mix into the crepe mixture.
Once combined, refrigerate batter for at least 2 hours.*

*Brush a crepe pan (or skillet) with oil or butter, then pour
off the excess. Heat the pan until drops of water dance in
the pan. Add ¼ cup of crepe batter to the pan and rotate the
pan so that the batter evenly covers the bottom of the pan.
Cook for about 60 seconds, then flip the crepe and cook for an
additional 30 seconds or until cooked. Stack crepes on a plate
until ready to use. Crepes freeze well for use at another time.*

MORNAY SAUCE:
4 ounces of butter
6 tablespoons of flour
3 to 3½ cups of milk
6 tablespoons grated Parmesan cheese
1 ounce heavy cream, whipped
Salt, to taste
Pepper, to taste

*In a skillet, melt the butter; add flour and stir until
absorbed. Stir in milk and cheese. Remove from
heat and fold in cream with seasonings.*

FILLING AND GARNISH:
1½ pounds roasted turkey breast, cut into cubes
12 ounces grated Parmesan cheese
16 strips of bacon, cooked and crumbled
2 large tomatoes, cut in small dice

*For Louis Browns, combine half the bacon and half of the cheese
in a bowl with the turkey. Spray an ovenproof casserole pan
with nonstick spray. Place a crepe in the ovenproof dish and
stuff with turkey filling, rolling each crepe. Repeat process
until all the crepes are filled. Cover the crepes with sauce.
Sprinkle with additional cheese and bacon and bake at 350°
until cooked, about 20–25 minutes. Broil at 450° until speckled
brown and bubbling, about 5 minutes. Remove from broiler,
top with bacon, cheese, and tomatoes and serve at once.*

Cornbread is a staple in the south. Cornbread can also be used
for Thanksgiving stuffing; in my opinion, cornbread makes
the best stuffing for Thanksgiving turkey and makes a great
Hot Brown. The recipe for cornbread muffins is adapted from
one found in the *Murray Woman's Club Cookbook*, 7th edition
(1991).

$\mathscr{T}$HE CORNBREAD BROWN

SERVES 4
8 corn muffins split in half, toasted (recipe below)
16 ounces roasted turkey
2 cups Mornay sauce (pp. 8, 10)
8 slices of bacon, cooked
2 Roma tomatoes, sliced in quarters
Parmesan cheese, grated

*Warm four plates. Pour ½ cup of Mornay sauce on each plate
and top with two corn muffins each cut in half. Top with turkey,
bacon and tomatoes. Sprinkle with Parmesan cheese. Serve.*

CORN MUFFINS:

1 cup corn meal

1 egg

1 teaspoon baking powder

1 tablespoon corn oil

1 heaping tablespoon flour

½ teaspoon baking soda

1 cup buttermilk

½ teaspoon salt

Preheat the oven to 450°, and place the corn muffin pan into the oven. Mix dry ingredients. Mix the egg with the wet ingredients. Mix the dry and wet ingredients together. Pull the pan from the oven, and pour the batter into the hot pan. Return the filled pan to the oven and cook for about 20 minutes at 450° or until done.

The Come Back Inn has two locations, one on each side of the Ohio River, and are open for dinner and available for caterings. The Italian-American restaurant features many classic Italian dishes and a wonderful take on the Hot Brown called the Italian Hot Brown. This recipe removes and replaces the bacon with pancetta and features Alfredo sauce. This is my interpretation of this wonderful adaptation.

HE ITALIAN HOT BROWN

SERVES 4–6

2 pounds smoked turkey, shredded

4 to 6 ciabatta bread buns

8 to 12 ounces of pancetta

4 Roma tomatoes, sliced

4 cups Alfredo sauce

Slice the ciabatta buns in half lengthwise. Place them in an ovenproof dish and toast under the broiler until they brown a little. Top with the shredded smoked turkey and Alfredo sauce. Return to the broiler until warm, then pull from the oven and add tomato slices and pancetta. Serve immediately.

If beer cheese is something that you enjoy—and who does not enjoy good beer cheese—perhaps you might try the Zesty Hot Brown. I found a similar recipe in the *More Hearthside Heritage Cookbook*, 1985 edition (green cover with blue script), which should not be confused with the 1972 edition (yellow cover with black script). The 1972 edition does contain a Hot Brown recipe that uses a broth-based cheese sauce. Both books, along with the 1965 edition, were sold to benefit the International Order of the King's Daughters and Sons. The Kentucky chapter holds a memorial luncheon to honor the Kentucky's own Jennie Carter Benedict (1860–1928), who is best known for the creation of Benedictine Cheese and author of *The Blue Ribbon Cookbook*. Benedict was a member of the order, evidenced by the Maltese Cross on her gravestone in Cave Hill Cemetery, Louisville.

# ZESTY HOT BROWN

½ pound cheddar cheese, grated
1 tablespoon butter
¼ teaspoon salt
½ teaspoon dry mustard
Pinch of cayenne
1 teaspoon paprika
½ cup ale or lager

1 egg, slightly beaten
3 drops Worcestershire sauce
1 pound turkey breast, roasted and sliced
8 bacon slices, cooked crisp
4 tomato slices
4 slices Texas toast, toasted

Cook the cheddar, butter, salt, dry mustard, cayenne and paprika together slowly in a heavy pan until the cheese melts. Stir occasionally. Slowly add the beer and the egg; stir constantly until thick. Add the Worcestershire sauce and stir. Place the toast on an ovenproof plate. Top the toast with turkey and cover with sauce. Place under the broiler for a few minutes to brown and remove from the oven. Add the tomato, then the bacon, and serve.

Have a big hungry crew to satisfy? Need a lot of Hot Browns? Try this recipe for making a large number of Hot Browns at one time. This recipe uses the modern convenience of canned soup to shorten the time making the sauce. This is an adapted recipe from *The Farmington Cookbook* (1979). Farmington is a historic house in Louisville that happens to be located behind Sullivan University's Louisville campus, and between I-264 (the Watterson Expressway) and a neighborhood; all three completely surround the property. The estate is a fraction of the plantation that it once was, but remains a calm center in the hustle and bustle of Louisville. Many of the original buildings still stand, and tours are conducted in the main house, which was built in 1810 from plans drawn by Thomas Jefferson. Abraham Lincoln visited Farmington in 1841 and was a lifelong friend of Joshua Speed, the son of John and Lucy Fry Speed, owners of the plantation at its completion, and brother to James Speed who served as the United States attorney general during Lincoln's presidency.

ℋOT BROWN SANDWICHES EN MASSE

SERVES 12

12 thick slices of turkey breast
24 slices of bacon
12 slices of bread (Texas toast)
12 slices of tomato
12–36 mushroom caps
4 cups Substitute Sauce Supreme (recipe below)
1 cup grated Parmesan cheese

Place bacon on a rimmed baking sheet and cook on bottom grid of a 400° oven until crisp. The timing of this will depend on the thickness of the bacon, but allow 6 to 8 minutes. Wrap the mushrooms in foil and cook in the oven while the bacon and the sandwiches cook. Drain the bacon on paper towels. Arrange the bread slices on the baking sheet right in the bacon fat, turning them on both sides to absorb it evenly. Put the baking sheet on the bottom rack and cook until the bread is toasted on the bottom, about 4 to 6 minutes. Remove, turn the bread over, and bake the other side until toasted, about 2 minutes. Place the turkey slices on each piece of bread and grind a little pepper over all. Combine sauce and Parmesan cheese. Cover each sandwich with the sauce. Return the pan to the upper half of the oven until the tops brown. Transfer to a serving platter and top each sandwich with a slice of tomato, 2 slices of bacon, and a mushroom (or two or three).

SUBSTITUTE SAUCE SUPREME:
2 cans cream of chicken soup
⅔ cup light cream
2 teaspoons lemon juice
Salt, to taste
Pepper, to taste
Combine and heat.

My father shared with me his love for hot dogs by taking me to James Coney Island in Houston, Texas, when I was a boy. There is nothing like a good hot dog. I once planned a trip around hot dogs. I traveled from Louisville to New York City. On the way to New York, I enjoyed my layover in Chicago's Midway Airport at Superdawg's. Once I was in New York, I ate at both Grey's Papaya and at Papaya King. On the return trip to Louisville, I enjoyed my layover in Atlanta's airport at the Varsity. Here is an ode to the hot dog and to the Hot Brown. Enjoy!

HE HOT BROWN DOG

SERVES 4
8 hot dog buns
8 hot dogs
8 small slices of roast turkey
8 slices of bacon, cooked
2 Roma tomatoes, sliced in rounds
2 cups Mornay sauce
4 ounces Parmesan cheese, grated

Toast the hot dog buns. Cook the hot dogs in a pan on the stove.
Line the hot dog buns with the turkey and a slice of bacon. Add
the hot dog. Add 2 ounces of sauce to the top of the hot dog,
top with tomato, and sprinkle with Parmesan cheese. Serve.

The Goose Creek Diner in Louisville featured a creative twist on the Hot Brown called the James Brown. The twist was a simple substitution—roast beef for the turkey. Many people know singer James Brown (1933–2006) as the "Godfather of Soul." With his big hair and distinctive voice and dance style, he was an incredible performer.

AMES BROWN

SERVES 4
4 slices Texas toast, toasted
24 ounces roast beef, sliced
2 cups Mornay sauce (pp. 8, 10; made with cream)
8 tomato slices
8 slices of bacon, cooked

Preheat the oven to 375°. Place the Texas toast on a sheet
pan. In a skillet, heat the roast beef until warm, about one
minute on each side. Place 6 ounces of the roast beef on
each slice of the Texas toast. Top each with Mornay sauce,
then with 2 tomato slices. Finally add the bacon slices.
Bake 5 to 10 minutes or until the Mornay sauce bubbles.

Hall's on the River, in Winchester, Kentucky (outside of Lexington), offers many delightful items to eat: beer cheese (which they also put on a burger, and sell packaged to go home), fried pickle planks, fried green tomatoes, lamb fries, and pimento cheese. They also have their own twist on the Hot Brown—the Seafood Hot Brown. I took this idea and created a seafood Hot Brown that you can create at home.

$\mathscr{T}$HE SEAFOOD HOT BROWN

SERVES 4

2 cups Parmesan Mornay sauce (pp. 8, 10)
8 slices Texas toast, toasted
4 5-ounce fillets of white crappie (or other fish)
4 tomato slices
Salt, to taste
Pepper, to taste
Parmesan cheese, grated
12 strips of bacon

Cook the fish in the oven until just cooked. For each Hot Brown, place 2 slices of toast in an ovenproof dish. Place the fish on top of the toast and cover with sauce. Sprinkle with additional cheese and broil until speckled brown and bubbling. Remove from broiler, place a tomato slice on top, and cross 2 strips of cooked bacon on top. Serve at once.

Kentucky native Chef Jonathan Lundy was nominated for a James Beard award and is a graduate of Johnson & Wales University. Chef Lundy elevates the Hot Brown to the next level with the use of brioche and scallops. Brioche is a rich egg-and-butter bread, which increases the richness of this dish, the Sea Scallop Hot Brown, so it should be served in small portions.[4]

$\mathscr{S}$EA SCALLOP HOT BROWN

SEA SCALLOP HOT BROWN SAUCE:
3 ounces of butter
4 tablespoons flour
2 cups heavy cream
2 cups shrimp stock
2 cups shredded white cheddar cheese
1 teaspoon salt
¼ teaspoon ground white pepper

In a small pan melt the butter, then add the flour to make a roux. Stir the mixture together for a few minutes but do not allow the roux to color. Add the shrimp stock into the roux and stir until you have a uniform sauce. Take the sauce off the burner, then add cream and cheese and stir until incorporated. Once the sauce comes together, refrigerate. The sauce should be made first and can be made up to three days in advance.

4 cups water
1 teaspoon sea salt
6 large sea scallops
6 cups ice
1 loaf unsliced brioche bread
¼ pound thinly sliced cooked country ham
4 cups Sea Scallop Hot Brown Sauce
12 cherry tomatoes

In a small pot, bring the water and salt to a boil. Submerge the scallops in the water and cook for about 3 minutes. Remove the pot from the heat and add 6 cups of ice to stop the cooking process. Once the scallops are cool, remove them from the water. Cut each scallop in half horizontally, then set aside.

Cook bacon until almost done (not crisp). Then slice bacon in thin strips. Cut the bread into 1-inch slices then toast. Slice off the crusts of the bread and cut the slices into quarters.

Assemble the Hot Browns by putting a small amount of sauce on the bread. Top with ham and sea scallops. Add a cross of bacon and more sauce. Refrigerate until ready to cook. Preheat oven to 400°. Slice the cherry tomatoes into small disks. Place the assembled Hot Browns in the oven for 6 minutes or until completely warmed. Remove from oven. Garnish with a cherry slice and serve.

Another option is to fix a Hot Brown pizza. Why not? Hometown Pizza in Louisville has the Hot Brown Pizza on the menu and the Louisville *Courier-Journal* featured a Hot Brown pizza in the April 20, 2011 main edition. This pizza recipe is an adaptation of the one featured in the pre-Derby article.

OT BROWN PIZZA

SERVES 4

2 premade 10-inch pizza shells
2 cups Mornay sauce
1 cup Parmesan cheese, shredded
½ cup Romano cheese, shredded
1 cup mozzarella cheese, shredded
1 cup turkey breast, roasted and diced

1 cup bacon, cooked and chopped
1 cup tomato, diced
1 tablespoon paprika
¼ cup parsley, chopped

Preheat oven to 400°. Pour 1 cup of Mornay sauce on each pizza shell, and top each with ½ cup Parmesan cheese and ½ cup mozzarella cheese. Add ½ cup diced turkey breast, ½ cup bacon, ½ cup tomatoes, ½ tablespoon paprika, and finally ¼ cup Romano cheese. Bake for 10 to 12 minutes or until golden brown on top and crust is set. Sprinkle with parsley. Allow the pizza to set for a minute before cutting. Serve and enjoy!

Dickie Brennan's Bourbon House in New Orleans is a wonderful place to relax and enjoy tasty food. I feel like I have a special connection to the Bourbon House because I attended elementary school about nine blocks away in the French Quarter and because I was inspired by a dinner at the Bourbon House to write *The Kentucky Bourbon Cookbook*. For the past four years, I have enjoyed judging food and cocktails at the Bourbon Classic in Louisville. Two years ago, Dickie Brennan's Bourbon House presented a Cajun Hot Brown to the judges. This is my version of their dish.

$\mathcal{C}$AJUN HOT BROWN

SERVES 4

2 cups Parmesan Mornay sauce (pp. 8, 10)
8 slices French bread, sliced and toasted
16 ounces smoked turkey breast
4 tomato slices
Salt, to taste
Pepper, to taste
Grated Parmesan cheese
4 slices of andouille sausage, cut in half

For each Hot Brown, place 2 slices of toasted French bread in an ovenproof dish. Place the turkey on top of the toast and cover with sauce. Sprinkle with additional cheese and broil until speckled brown and bubbling. Remove from broiler, place a tomato slice on top, cross two strips of andouille on top, and serve at once.

Magnolia Suddeth won top honors at the 2015 Kentucky State Fair and a $2,000 prize. When she won, Suddeth was a 12-year-old who attended Noe Middle School in Louisville, Kentucky. The following is an adapted version of Suddeth's recipe.

$\mathscr{T}$HE SPAM BROWN

SERVES 6
1½ tablespoons butter
1½ tablespoons all-purpose flour
1½ cups whole milk or heavy cream
½ teaspoon hot pepper sauce
½ teaspoon Worcestershire sauce
1 cup white cheddar cheese, shredded
1 2-ounce can SPAM Classic, cut into 6 slices
6 slices dense white bread or oatmeal bread, toasted
6 large tomato slices
12 slices, cooked bacon
Black pepper, to taste
Fresh parsley, chopped

*In a large saucepan, melt the butter. Add flour, heat, then
stir over medium heat until lightly browned and bubbly,
about 2 minutes. Add milk or cream, hot pepper sauce, and
Worcestershire sauce. Heat and stir over medium heat until
sauce is thickened. Remove the sauce from the heat and
stir in the cheese until melted. Keep warm and set aside.*

*Preheat oven to 350°. In large skillet, heat SPAM Classic
until lightly browned on both sides. In an ovenproof baking
dish, arrange toasted bread slices. Top with SPAM Classic
and tomato slices. Sprinkle black pepper over the tomatoes.
Spoon prepared cheese sauce over each. Place in oven
and heat for about 5 minutes or until lightly brown. Top
each with 2 slices of bacon and chopped fresh parsley.*

Like James Graham Brown, Chef John Castro grew up in Indiana. After graduating high school, he attended the Culinary Institute of American in Hyde Park, New York, before moving home, this time to the south side of the Ohio River. During his career, he served as executive chef at Hassenour's in Louisville and then joined Sullivan University's NCHS as a chef-instructor. Eventually, he would be named as the executive chef at Winston's, the restaurant on campus at Sullivan University—a position he would hold for eighteen years. During his tenure at Winston's, his brother, Chef Joe Castro, was the executive chef at the Brown Hotel. John was always asked if he had a Hot Brown on the menu, and he would always direct people to the Brown Hotel for the genuine experience. Eventually, he developed a dish which he called the "Not Brown." Here is my interpretation of John's masterful gastronomic pun.

OT BROWN

SERVES 4

8 tablespoons butter

2½ cups flour

3 cups milk

2 cups plus ½ cup Gruyere or Swiss cheese, shredded

2 cups cream

2 whole green tomatoes

4 eggs

2 cups panko bread crumbs

4 cups vegetable oil

1 pound (35–40) rock shrimp

¾ pound Dungeness crabmeat

4 cups baby spinach

12 cherry tomatoes, halved
8 slices bacon, fried and cut into small pieces
8 large shrimp, cooked (optional for garnish)

In a pan, melt 4 tablespoons of the butter. Add ½ cup of flour. Stir constantly until mixture begins to take some color, smells slightly nutty and forms a blond roux. Incorporate 3 cups of milk into roux and whisk to combine. Bring to a simmer and allow to simmer until mixture thickens enough to coat the back of a spoon. Add 2 cups of cheese and 2 cups of cream. Continue to whisk until all cheese has melted. Strain through a fine mesh strainer. Store in refrigerator until needed. Can be made several days in advance.

Slice green tomatoes to ¼-inch thickness, making at least 8 slices. Season the remaining 2 cups of flour with salt and pepper. In a separate bowl, whisk the eggs with a touch of water. Put the panko bread crumbs in a third bowl. Coat each tomato slice in seasoned flour, the egg wash, and bread crumbs until coated. Store in refrigerator until needed. Can be made up to one day ahead.

Pour vegetable oil into a pot and heat to 350° (use a thermometer to measure temperature). Be very careful, as oil is both very hot and flammable. Deep-fry coated tomatoes in oil until crispy on all sides. Remove, season with salt and pepper and drain on paper towel. Add the remaining 4 tablespoons of butter to large sauté pan, and heat. Add rock shrimp to pan and sauté until almost done. Add 12 ounces of crab to pan, and sauté until both the crab and shrimp are thoroughly cooked. Add 1 quart of cheese sauce and spinach. Season with salt and pepper, and stir. Continue cooking until the spinach has begun to wilt.

In four separate ovenproof bowls, place approximately ⅛ of the sauce into the bottom of each bowl. Place 1 green tomato slice in the center. Top tomato with a mound of cooked shrimp/crab/spinach. Place second green tomato slice directly on top of seafood, forming a tower. Divide remaining sauce among the four bowls, pouring over and around the green tomatoes. Top with cherry tomato halves, bacon, and large shrimp (optional), and sprinkle with ½ cup Gruyere cheese. Broil approximately 3 minutes, until cheese begins to bubble and brown.

The Monkey Wrench in Louisville, Kentucky, is a cool bar with classic cocktails and a smart menu. One of the featured items is the Kentucky Tot Brown. As the name implies, tater tots are covered in lots of hot brown goodness, and they are served like nachos where everything tops the chips. Here is my interpretation of this menu masterpiece.

KENTUCKY TOT BROWN

SERVES 1

4 ounces tater tots, cooked according to the directions
2 ounces sliced roasted turkey breast, chopped into bite-size pieces
2 strips of bacon, cooked and chopped
½ tomato, diced
1 cup Mornay sauce (pp. 8, 10)
Grated Parmesan cheese

Cook the tater tots according to the directions on the package. Place the tater tots into an ovenproof plate. Cover the tots with the turkey and the Mornay sauce. Bake in

the oven for a few minutes until the dish is hot and the
cheese begins to bubble. Pull the plate from the oven and
top with bacon, tomato, and Parmesan cheese. Serve.

Patti's 1880's Settlement is located in the small town of Grand Rivers, Kentucky, near Land Between the Lakes National Recreation Area. Patti's offers customers an incredible selection of entrees and "Patti's Oldies but Goodies" which includes a traditional Kentucky Hot Brown and a ground beef riff on the Hot Brown called the Patti Brown. This is my version of the Patti Brown.

ATTI BROWN

SERVES 4
4 slices thick white bread
2 pounds ground beef
12 ounces mushrooms, sliced
2 cups cheddar Mornay sauce (pp. 8, 10)
4 ounces kettle-style potato chips
2 tablespoons butter
Salt, to taste
Pepper, to taste

Start by adding salt and pepper to the ground beef and mix until incorporated. Form the ground beef into four large round patties. Slice the mushrooms. Melt the butter in a sauté pan, add the mushrooms, and then cook until done. Set the mushrooms aside. Cook the patties on the grill, in the oven, or in a pan until the ground beef is cooked to your desired doneness. Toast the white bread. Place one piece of toasted white bread on an ovenproof dish for each Patti

Brown. Place the ground beef patty on top of the bread then
cover with mushrooms. Cover the sandwich with ½ cup of
Mornay sauce and place the dish under the broiler. When the
dish begins to brown, pull the dish from the oven and add
one ounce of potato chips to the top of the dish and serve.

When my son Michael was eight years old, I taught him how to make scrambled eggs. Over the next year, he became obsessed with the many ways to cook eggs: fried, over easy, poached, etc., until one day he announced, "I want to be a chef." I asked him what cuisine would be his specialty and he replied, "Eggs!" Encouraging his enthusiasm, I asked what else he would cook. "Just eggs." "Are you going to open a breakfast restaurant?" I asked. "No—I am going to open a restaurant that serves eggs." "Your restaurant needs to serve more than eggs." "No, Dad. My restaurant is going to serve only eggs." A few months later I ran into a former student, J. J. Kingery, who was named the executive chef at a new restaurant in Louisville. I congratulated him and asked, "What kind of cuisine?" "Eggs," he responded. "Excuse me?" "Eggs." I arranged for Michael to eat at Wild Eggs which is located near Suburban Hospital (of course, now they have several other locations around town). Chef JJ visited the table, and I explained Michael's idea while I ate a little crow that morning. The Wild Eggs menu includes other breakfast and lunch items as well as their many egg-inspired dishes. That morning I ate the Kelsey "KY" Brown which is based on the Hot Brown. Michael relished that his idea for a restaurant was operational. In a 2016 *USA Today* "10 Best" readers' poll, the Kelsey "KY" Brown beat out the original served at the Brown Hotel in the Hot Brown category! This is my version of the dish.

$\mathcal{K}$ELSEY "KY" BROWN

SERVES 4

4 large slices sourdough bread, lightly toasted
16 ounces roasted turkey, sliced
8 slices of bacon, cooked
1 large tomato, diced
2 cups white cheddar Mornay sauce (pp. 8, 10)
4 eggs (fried, over easy, or poached)
Smoked paprika

For each breakfast sandwich, place the toast onto an oven safe plate and top with the bacon, then the turkey. Cover each sandwich with ½ cup Mornay sauce and place the plates back into the oven. Cook the eggs. Pull the plates from the oven, and place the eggs on the Mornay-covered turkey. Garnish with diced tomatoes and paprika. Serve.

The Brown Hotel and the Mayfair Hotel (since 2014, the Magnolia Hotel St. Louis) are both on the United States National Register of Historic Places. The Brown Hotel was built in 1923 in Louisville, Kentucky, while the Mayfair Hotel was built during 1924 in St. Louis, Missouri. The Brown Hotel has sixteen floors while the Mayfair Hotel has eighteen floors. The outside designs of both hotels have many similarities. The Hot Brown was created at the Brown Hotel by Chef Fred Schmidt in 1926, and the Prosperity Sandwich was created by chef and executive steward Eduard Voegeli at the Mayfair Hotel.[5] There are also many similarities between the hotels' Hot Brown and Prosperity sandwiches. Even though some claim that the Prosperity Sandwich was created in the 1920s, this seems unlikely. The Hot Brown takes its name from the hotel where it was first created; the name for the Prosperity Sandwich may have been a political statement. After the stock market crash of 1929, Republican president Herbert Hoover implied that "prosperity was just around the corner." Even though he may never have said those words, the phrase was attributed to Hoover and was used by the Democratic Party as an ironic attack. If this is where the Prosperity Sandwich gets its name, the sandwich would most likely have been created in the early 1930s when Hoover was still claiming quick economic recovery, but most people no longer believe that to be true. Others claim that the Prosperity Sandwich claims the name from the use of rich ingredients.

ROSPERITY SANDWICH

Mayfair Hotel, St. Louis, Missouri

SERVES 2–4

2 cups whole or 2 percent milk

¼ cup (½ stick) unsalted butter or margarine

¼ cup all-purpose flour

½ cup plus 1 tablespoon grated Parmesan cheese, divided

½ cup grated mild cheddar cheese

Salt, optional

Ground black pepper

4 thick slices whole wheat or other hearty bread, lightly toasted

4–6 ounces sliced baked turkey

4–6 ounces sliced ham

2–4 slices bacon, cooked until crisp

For a consistently smooth sauce, make sure to measure out cold milk. Set aside and keep the milk cool until ready to use. Melt butter in large saucepan over medium-low heat. Do not let butter brown. Slowly sprinkle flour into pan, whisking constantly until mixture forms a paste. Cook for about 2 minutes over medium-low heat, still whisking constantly, and don't allow the paste to gain color. Slowly whisk in cold milk; cook over medium-low heat 2 to 3 minutes, whisking frequently, until slightly thickened. Remove from heat; whisk in ½ cup Parmesan, then stir in cheddar until the sauce is smooth. Then add salt and pepper to taste. For each serving, place both slices of bread side by side on an ovenproof plate and top with slices of turkey, then ham. Pour on half to three-quarters of the sauce, covering the bread and meat completely. Sprinkle with the remaining 1 tablespoon Parmesan. For lighter servings, place 1 slice of bread on each of four ovenproof plates; top each with 2 ounces of turkey, 2 ounces of ham, and half of the cheese sauce. Sprinkle with Parmesan cheese. Place sandwich or sandwiches under a hot broiler until sauce is brown and bubbly, 3 to 5 minutes. Garnish with bacon and serve immediately.

In 1934, Frank Blandi, a restaurateur in Pittsburgh, Pennsylvania, created the Devonshire Sandwich when he was at the Stratford Club in Millvale.[6] He named the sandwich after Devonshire Street which was near the club. Imitation is the best form of flattery—reviewing this recipe leaves little doubt that the recipe for the Devonshire Sandwich is very close to the Hot Brown.

$\mathscr{T}$URKEY DEVONSHIRE SANDWICH

Stratford Club, Pittsburgh, Pennsylvania

6 tablespoons butter
1 cup flour
¼ cup grated mild cheddar
1 pint chicken broth
1 pint hot milk
1 teaspoon salt
For each sandwich:
1 slice toasted thick white bread
3 slices crisp cooked bacon
5 thin slices turkey breast or shredded leftover turkey
Parmesan cheese to garnish
Paprika to garnish

CREAM SAUCE:
*Melt the butter in saucepan, add the flour, and whisk.
Add the chicken broth and milk while whisking to ensure
a smooth sauce. Bring to boil and cook over reduced heat
for 20 minutes while stirring often; then add cheese and
salt. Stir again to allow the cheese to melt evenly in the
sauce. Remove from heat and cool to lukewarm.*

FOR EACH SANDWICH:
Preheat oven to 450°.

*In a pan, place 1 slice of toast per sandwich or if you have
single serving baking dishes, use them. Add the bacon, then the
turkey, and cover completely with cream sauce. Sprinkle with
Parmesan cheese and paprika. Bake 10–15 minutes until golden.*

FOUR

Kentucky Hotel Cuisine

THERE WAS A TIME WHEN the Brown Hotel was gastronom-
ically known for more than just the Hot Brown. Chef Fred
K. Schmidt, who invented the Hot Brown, also invented the
Cold Brown. Marion Flexner reports the "Brown Sandwich
(cold)" in her classic cookbook, *Out of Kentucky Kitchens*. The
Cold Brown is also featured in *The Derby Party Cooking Clinic*
by Barbara Harper-Bach and *The Cooking Book and Traditional
Recipes*, compiled by the Junior League of Louisville.[1] Harper-
Bach's version substitutes "soft sour dough bread" slices with
the crusts removed, adds sliced Swiss cheese, is served with
a side of bread and butter pickles, and features a more con-
servative amount of Thousand Island dressing. The Junior
League recipe substitutes Russian dressing for the Thousand
Island dressing. While the two dressings are similar, shar-
ing the same mayonnaise and tomato base, Russian dressing
is spicier, with horseradish and hot sauce, while Thousand
Island is sweet. Also, the Junior League garnishes this sandwich with "black caviar." This is Flexner's version of the Cold
Brown.

THE COLD BROWN

1 thin slice rye bread, crust removed
Thin slices baked chicken or turkey
Bibb or leaf lettuce to cover bread
1 slice ripe tomato, peeled (large)
1 egg, hard boiled and sliced in rings
Thousand Island dressing to top sandwich

This is an open-faced sandwich. To make it, place the bread on the salad plate. Butter it lightly if you wish. Cover with the lettuce, then the meat, then the tomato (cut ½-inch thick). Frame the tomato with the egg circles. Surround with more Bibb lettuce leaves or shredded leaf lettuce. Pass Thousand Island dressing to douse all over sandwich.

Another culinary dish the Brown Hotel was known for was Chicken Chow Mein. The recipe is listed in the 1984 edition of The Woman's Club of Louisville Cookbook, *Favorite Fare II*, which also lists a recipe for the Hot Brown on the next page.[2]

CHICKEN CHOW MEIN
Brown Hotel Way

SERVES 12
2–3 pound hens, boiled and stock reserved
2 cups fresh mushrooms, sliced
3 onions, sliced
3 celery stalks, sliced
Oil
10 cups chicken stock

1½ cups soy sauce
1 cup bamboo shoots, sliced
1 cup water chestnuts, sliced
1 14-ounce can bean sprouts
1½ cups cornstarch
Salt, to taste
Pepper, to taste
Fried Chinese noodles
Garnish (recipe below)

Cut the cooked chicken into strips; reserve 1 cup for garnish. Sauté mushrooms, onions, and celery in oil for a few minutes. Add stock and soy sauce; cook for a while but leave vegetables crisp. Add bamboo shoots, water chestnuts, bean sprouts, and chicken. Bring to a boil and thicken with cornstarch mixed with stock. Season with salt and pepper. Serve over noodles and sprinkle garnish over the top.

GARNISH:
Reserved chicken
2 shredded leeks
Toasted cashew nuts, chopped
1 cup shredded pancake (recipe below)
Mix well and sprinkle over the Chow Mein before
    serving.
Pancake for shredding
2 eggs
2 tablespoons milk
2 tablespoons flour

Mix well and pour into a greased medium-hot skillet that is large enough to make a very thin pancake. Turn to brown on both sides. Remove from skillet and shred into thin strips.

Muhammad Ali—"The Greatest"—was born Cassius M. Clay Jr. in Louisville, Kentucky, in 1942. During his lifetime, he would establish himself as the best boxer of all time. He won the Olympic Gold medal in 1960 and the World Heavyweight title four years later, in 1964, after which he converted to Islam and changed his name to Muhammad Ali. The title was stripped from him two years later, in 1966, for refusing to be drafted into the United States military. Ali cited religious beliefs but was arrested and found guilty of draft evasion. The verdict was overturned on appeal by the United States Supreme Court. He would win the title back in 1974 and again in 1978—he remains the only three-time heavyweight champion! After retiring, he devoted his life to religious and charitable work. Ali was diagnosed with Parkinson's disease in 1984. He died in 2016 and is buried in Louisville's Cave Hill Cemetery. Ali was known for saying, "I float like a butterfly and sting like a bee,"—much like this recipe!

MUHAMMAD ALI SMASH

- 1 ounce agave nectar
- 1 ounce Pama liqueur
- 1 ounce Rittenhouse Rye or bourbon brand of your choice
- 1 lemon wedge
- 6 mint leaves

Muddle 1 lemon wedge with 6 fresh mint leaves.
Add liquors above; add crushed ice and serve!

There are many hotels in Louisville's downtown. In fact, there are more popping up all the time. The other historic grand hotel in the downtown area is the Seelbach Hotel which is located on Fourth Street and Muhammad Ali Boulevard. The Seelbach opened in 1905 and like the Brown Hotel, the Seelbach is named for its founders, Otto and Louis Seelbach. Over the years, the Seelbach Hotel played host to many famous people, including F. Scott Fitzgerald, culinary icons Julia Child and Wolfgang Puck, nine US presidents dating back to President William Howard Taft in 1911 and including, most recently, George W. Bush in 2002, and mob icons Al Capone, Lucky Luciano, and Dutch Schultz. With all this history, the idea of discovering a long-lost preprohibition cocktail seemed plausible when Adam Segar, the director of the hotel's restaurant announced the discovery in 1995. The cocktail is a solid mixture of Cointreau, bitters, bourbon, and sparkling wine—a rediscovered classic cocktail, very like a champagne cocktail. However, Segar admitted in 2016 to the *New York Times* that he made the whole cocktail up, literally and figuratively. During the two decades that Segar kept his secret, the cocktail became a classic.

HE SEELBACH COCKTAIL

1 ounce bourbon
½ ounce Cointreau
7 dashes of Angostura bitters
7 dashes of Peychaud's bitters
5 ounces sparkling wine
Orange twist

Prepare a champagne flute with water and crushed ice. Once chilled, pour out the water and ice mixture. Add the bourbon, Cointreau, and bitters to the glass, then top off with sparkling wine. Garnish with an orange twist.

Patricia Wilson was in a beautiful blue dress when she fell to her death down an elevator shaft at the Seelbach Hotel in the 1930s. Some say it was suicide because she seemed distressed when seen earlier in the day. Since then, her spirit has been seen wandering the hall on the eighth floor. Bar manager Eron Plevan, a former seminarian, created a drink to honor the Lady in Blue. Plevan based this drink on a White Lady which is a gin-based drink.

HE LADY IN BLUE

1½ ounces gin (Bombay Sapphire)
¾ ounce lemon juice
½ ounce simple syrup
2–3 drops orange flower water
½ bar spoon crème de violet
½ ounce Blue Curaçao
Edible flowers to garnish

Chill a cocktail glass with ice and water. Pour the gin, lemon juice, simple syrup, orange flower water, and crème de violet into a Boston shaker and add ice. Shake until the tin begins to frost. Empty the cocktail glass. Strain the cocktail into the chilled glass. Add the Blue Curaçao off to the side of the drink so that the "blue dress" appears. Serve.

NOTES

1. The Hot Brown

1. *Larousse Gastronomique*, (New York: Clarkson Potter, 2001), 375; John E. Kleber, ed., *The Kentucky Encyclopedia* (Lexington: University Press of Kentucky, 1992), 443; John E. Kleber, *The Louisville Encyclopedia* (Lexington: University Press of Kentucky, 2000), 306, 404.

2. Kleber, The Kentucky Encyclopedia, 443; Marion Flexner, *Out of Kentucky Kitchens* (New York: Bramhall House, 1949), 31–32.

3. Marion Flexner, *Out of Kentucky Kitchens* (New York: Bramhall House, 1949), 31–32; Springfield Woman's Club, *A Tasting Tour through Washington County Kentucky* (Olathe, KS: Cookbook Publishers, 1987), 139; Michael Edwards Masters, *Hospitality—Kentucky Style: Kentucky Heritage Grand Tour Kentucky Fine Food & Spirits* (Bardstown, KY: Equine Writer's Press, 2003), 196; Charles Patteson, *Charles Patteson's Kentucky Cooking* (New York: Harper & Row, 1988), 151; Dorothea C. Cooper, ed., *Kentucky Hospitality: A 200-Year Tradition* (Louisville: Kentucky Federation of Women's Clubs, 1976), 101; Patteson, *Charles Patteson's Kentucky Cooking*, 151.

4. Kleber, *The Louisville Encyclopedia*, 306.

5. Elaine Corn, *The Courier-Journal* (Louisville, KY), January 6, 1985, Late Kentucky Ed., p. 18.

6. Sarah R. Labensky and Alan M. Hause, *On Cooking: A Textbook of Culinary Fundamentals*, 2nd ed., (Upper Saddle River, NJ: Prentice-Hall, 1999), 197.; Auguste Escoffier, *The Escoffier Cook Book* (New York: Crown, 1969), 21; Julia Child, Louisette Bertholle, and Simone Beck, *Mastering the Art of French Cooking*, Vol. 1 (New York: Alfred A. Knopf, 1985), 61.

7. James Peterson, *Cooking: 600 Recipes, 1500 Photographs, One Kitchen Education* (Berkeley, CA: Ten Speed Press, 2007), 341–342.

8. Richard Hougen, *Look No Further* (New York: Abingdon, 1955), 194; Richard Hougen, *Cooking with Hougen* (New York: Abingdon, 1960), 82; Richard Hougen, *More Hougen Favorites* (New York: Abingdon, 1971), 74.

9. Hougen, *More Hougen Favorites*, 74.

2. People, Places, and Things

1. Oressa Teagarden, *Courier-Journal* (Louisville, KY), March 25, 1939, p. 20.

2. Elaine Corn, *Courier-Journal* (Louisville, KY), January 6, 1985, Late Kentucky edition, 18.

3. Leslie Ellis, *Courier-Journal* (Louisville, KY), May 4, 1999, Kentucky edition, 3.

3. Recipes

1. Elaine Corn, *The Courier-Journal* (Louisville, KY), January 6, 1985, Late Kentucky Ed., 18.

2. Sister Cities of Louisville, accessed 6/16/17, http://www.sclou .org/city.

3. David Dominé, *Adventures in New Kentucky Cooking* (Kuttawa, KY: McClanahan, 2007), 44–45; *Derby Entertaining: Traditional Kentucky Recipes* (Kuttawa, KY: McClanahan, 2008), 30.

4. Jonathan Lundy, *Jonathan's Bluegrass Table: Redefining Kentucky Cuisine* (Louisville, KY: Butler Books, 2009), 88–89; David Dominé, *111 Fabulous Food Finds* (Kuttawa, KY: McClanahan, 2011), 161.

5. Patricia Treacy, *The Grand Hotels of St. Louis* (Mount Pleasant, SC: Arcadia, 2005), 72.

6. *Pittsburgh Post-Gazette*, December 11, 1991, 18.

4. Kentucky Hotel Cuisine

1. John E. Kleber, ed. *The Louisville Encyclopedia* (Lexington: University Press of Kentucky, 2000), 306; Marion Flexner, *Out of Kentucky Kitchens* (New York: Bramhall House, 1949), 31; Barbara Harper-Bach, *The Derby Party Cooking* Clinic (Barbara Harper-Bach, 2013), 66; Junior League of Louisville, *The Cooking Book and Traditional Recipes* (Louisville, KY: Junior League, 1978), 73.

2. Woman's Club of Louisville, *Favorite Fare II* (Louisville, KY: Woman's Club of Louisville, 1984), 10.

BIBLIOGRAPHY

Benedict, Jennie C. *The Blue Ribbon Cook Book*. Lexington: University
    Press of Kentucky, 2008.

Bicentennial Cookbook. Leawood, KS: Circulation Service, 1989.

Cabbage Patch: Famous Kentucky Recipes. Louisville, KY: Gateway Press,
    1956.

Child, Julia, Louisette Bertholle, and Simone Beck. *Mastering the Art of
    French Cooking*. Vol. 1. New York: Alfred A. Knopf, 1985.

The Cincinnati Cook Book. Cincinnati, OH: The Co-operative Society of
    The Children's Hospital, 1967.

Cooper, Dorothea C., ed. *Kentucky Hospitality: A 200-Year Tradition*.
    Louisville: The Kentucky Federation of Women's Clubs, 1976.

Derby Entertaining: Traditional Kentucky Recipes. Kuttawa, KY:
    McClanahan, 2008.

Dominé, David. *Adventures in New Kentucky Cooking*. Kuttawa, KY:
    McClanahan, 2007.

Dominé, David. *111 Fabulous Food Finds: Best Bites in the Bluegrass*.
    Kuttawa, KY: McClanahan, 2011.

Dominé, David. *Splash of Bourbon Kentucky's Spirit*. Kuttawa, KY:
    McClanahan, 2010.

Donahoe, Betty Jane. *How to Boil Water*. Ashtabula, OH: River City
    Publishers, 1972.

Escoffier, Auguste. *The Escoffier Cook Book*. New York: Crown, 1969.

The Farmington Cookbook. Louisville, KY: Farmington, 1979

Finley, John, ed. *The Courier-Journal Kentucky Cookbook*. Louisville, KY:
    Courier-Journal and Louisville Times Company, 1985.

Flexner, Marion. *Out of Kentucky Kitchens*. New York: Bramhall House,
    1949.

Fritschner, Sarah. *Sarah Fritschner's Holidays: Menus and Recipes for the
    Fall Holiday Season*. Louisville, KY: Butler Books, 2004.

Godbey, Marty. *Dining in Historic Kentucky*. Kuttawa, KY: McClanahan,
    1992.

Harper-Bach, Barbara. *The Derby Party Cooking Clinic*. Barbara Harper-
    Bach, 2013.

Hayes, Irene. *What's Cooking in Kentucky*. Ft. Mitchell, KY: T. I. Hayes, 1994.

Hot Browne. Louisville, KY: Harvey Browne Memorial Presbyterian Church, 1984.

Hot Browne: A Second Helping. Lenexa, KS: Cookbook Publishers, 2003.

Hougen, Richard T. *Cooking with Hougen*. New York: Abingdon, 1960.

Hougen, Richard T. *Look No Further*. New York: Abingdon, 1955.

Hougen, Richard T. *More Hougen Favorites*. New York: Abingdon, 1971.

Junior League of Louisville. *The Cooking Book and Traditional Recipes*. Louisville, KY: Junior League, 1978.

Kleber, John E., ed. *The Kentucky Encyclopedia*. Lexington: University Press of Kentucky, 1992.

Kleber, John E., ed. *The Louisville Encyclopedia*. Lexington: University Press of Kentucky, 2000.

Labensky, Sarah R., and Alan M. Hause. *On Cooking: A Textbook of Culinary Fundamentals*. 2nd ed. Upper Saddle River, NJ: Prentice-Hall, 1999.

Librarie Larouuse. *Larousse Gastronomique*. New York: Clarkson Potter, 2001.

Lundy, Jonathan. *Jonathan's Bluegrass Table: Redefining Kentucky Cuisine*. Louisville, KY: Butler Books, 2009.

Marshall, Lillian. *The Courier-Journal & Times Cookbook*. Louisville, KY: Courier-Journal and Louisville Times Company, 1971.

Masters, Michael Edwards. *Hospitality – Kentucky Style: Kentucky Heritage Grand Tour, Kentucky Fine Food & Spirits*. Bardstown, KY: Equine Writer's Press, 2003.

Miss Patti's Cook Book. Kuttawa, KY: McClanahan, 1997.

More Favorites from First. New Orleans: First Presbyterian Church, 2013.

More Hearthside Heritage Cookbook. Shelbyville, KY: The Kingsway Circle of the International Order of the King's Daughters and Sons, 1985.

Murray Woman's Club. *Murray Woman's Club Cookbook*. Murray, KY: Quickprint of Murray, 1991.

Patteson, Charles. *Charles Patteson's Kentucky Cooking*. With Craig Emerson. New York: Harper & Row, 1988.

Peterson, James. *Cooking: 600 Recipes, 1500 Photographs, One Kitchen Education*. Berkeley, CA: Ten Speed Press, 2007.

Rankin, Jane Lee. *Cookin' Up A Storm: The Life and Recipes of Annie Johnson*. New York: Grace, 1998.

Schmid, Albert W. A. *The Kentucky Bourbon Cookbook*. Lexington: University Press of Kentucky, 2010.

Settle, Cherry, Tommy Settle, and Edward G. Klemm Jr. *The Claudia Sanders Dinner House of Shelbyville, Kentucky, Cookbook*. Louisville, KY: Courier Graphics, 1979.

Springfield Woman's Club. *A Tasting Tour through Washington County Kentucky*. Olathe, KS: Cookbook Publishers, 1987.

Thompson, Sharon. *Flavors of Kentucky*. Kuttawa, KY: McClanahan, 2006.

Treacy, Patricia. *The Grand Hotels of St. Louis*. Mount Pleasant, SC: Arcadia, 2005.

Woman's Club of Louisville. *Favorite Fare II*. Louisville, KY: Woman's Club of Louisville, 1984.

Women's Auxiliary to the Jefferson County Medical Society. *Prescriptions for Cooks*. Vol 2. Louisville, KY: Women's Auxiliary to the Jefferson County Medical Society, 1971.

Women's Hospital Auxiliary. *Woodford Recipes*. Louisville, KY: Grimes Press, 1967.

ALBERT W. A. SCHMID is award-winning author of several books, including *The Kentucky Bourbon Cookbook, The Manhattan Cocktail: A Modern Guide to the Whiskey Classic, The Old Fashioned: An Essential Guide to the Original Whiskey Cocktail,* and *The Beverage Manager's Guide to Wines, Beers, and Spirits.*

Milton Keynes UK
Ingram Content Group UK Ltd.
UKHW020610280723
425941UK00002B/16

9 781684 350056